LINDSAY/LINDSEY
Royalty Connections

from CHARLEMAGNE to

KINGS OF SCOTLAND

Compiled by

Betty Jewell Durbin Carson

DAR Member #832584

HERITAGE BOOKS

2026

HERITAGE BOOKS

AN IMPRINT OF HERITAGE BOOKS, INC.

Books, CDs, and more—Worldwide

For our listing of thousands of titles see our website
at
www.HeritageBooks.com

Published 2026 by
HERITAGE BOOKS, INC.
Publishing Division
5810 Ruatan Street
Berwyn Heights, MD 20740

International Standard Book Number
Paperbound: 978-0-7884-3539-3

Descendants of Charlemagne

Generation 1

1. CHARLEMAGNE [1] was born on 02 Apr 742 AD. He died on 28 Jan 813/14 AD. He married Hildegarde in 771 AD in Aix-la-Chapelle. She was born in 758 AD. She died on 30 Apr 783 AD.

   Notes for Charlemagne:
   King of the Franks, 768-841, Emperor of the West, 800-814, crowned Emperor at Rome on Christmas Day 800 by Pope Leo, III. Married Princess Hildegarde of Swabia, as third wife. Charlemagne carried on incessant wars, extending his domains and spreading Christianity. He was sagacious, energetic and viligant as a ruler and commander. He was succeeded by his only surviving son, Louis I.
   Sources: The Hon. Vicary Gibbs, *The Complete Peerage of England, Scotland, Ireland, Great Britain and The United Kingdom*, (London: The St. Catherine Press, 1913), Vol. III, pp. 507-517; James Balfour Paul, *The Scots Peerage,* (Edinburgh: David Douglas). Vol. 1, 1904.

   Born: c. 742
   Died: January 28, 814
   Aachen (now in Germany)
   Frankish king and ruler

   Charlemagne, or Charles the Great, was king of the Franks between 768 and 814, and emperor of the West between 800 and 814. He founded the Holy Roman Empire, strengthened European

Generation 1 (cont.)

economic and political life, and promoted the cultural revival known as the Carolingian Renaissance. Charlemagne's rule greatly influenced Europe's push to create a unique civilization different from that of Rome or other ancient empires.

Early life
Charlemagne, the son of Pepin the Short and Bertrada, was born in 742. Although his parents married before his brother Carloman was born, they were not legally married at the time of Charlemagne's birth, and he was thus thought to be illegitimate (born out of wedlock). In 741 Pepin had become mayor of the palace, and in 751 he deposed (removed from office) the last Merovingian king and was declared king of the Franks, a powerful Germanic tribe that lived in the region today known as France. Little is known about Charlemagne's childhood. In 754, however, he participated in the ceremony where Pope Stephen II appointed Pepin king. Charlemagne also joined Pepin on many military campaigns.

When Pepin died in October 768, Charlemagne and Carloman were both proclaimed king and were to rule the kingdom together. In the division of the realm, however, Carloman received a larger and richer portion. Under these circumstances relations between the brothers turned sour. But Carloman died unexpectedly in 771, leaving Charlemagne the

Generation 1 (cont.)

sole ruler of the entire kingdom.

Territorial expansion
Charlemagne moved aggressively, especially in Italy, to remove those who threatened his power. He immediately attacked and defeated King Desiderius of the Lombards. Shortly thereafter Charlemagne was crowned king of the Lombards at Pavia. The Frankish conquest of Italy-first of Lombardy in the north and later Benevento in the south-brought new wealth and people into his kingdom.

During his Italian operations Charlemagne also declared war against the Saxons, a Germanic tribe who threatened the northeastern frontier of Francia. Begun in 772, this cruel and bitter war finally ended in 804. Francia absorbed the land of Saxony and enforced the Christian religion on the Saxon tribes.

On his eastern frontier Charlemagne defeated Tassilo, the duke of Bavaria. To his empire Charlemagne added the Bavarian duchy, or territory controlled by a duke. He divided the western portion of the duchy into counties, each controlled by a count loyal to the king.

Further to the east the major power and ultimate threat to the Frankish realm was the vast Slavic kingdom of the Avars, or Huns, an Asiatic tribe

Generation 1 (cont.)

that had settled along the upper Danube River. Between 791 and 795 Charlemagne crushed the power of the Avars and added their kingdom as a state. This victory opened the entire Danubian Plain to German colonization and the eastern expansion of Christianity-the beginning of the Drang nach Osten, or push to the East.

Holy Roman Empire
By 800 Charlemagne had succeeded in greatly extending his power while crushing several enemies. He ruled all of the Christianized western provinces, except the British Isles, that had once been part of the Roman Empire. As the sworn protector of the Church, Charlemagne was in fact the political master of Rome itself. The papacy, or office of the pope, also recognized Charlemagne's power. The pope crowned Charlemagne Holy Roman Emperor on Christmas Day, 800.

Charlemagne attempted to create unity and harmony within his vast realm and to support laws and promote learning that would achieve his goals of the empire. Charlemagne, in contrast to his Merovingian predecessors (who constantly traveled throughout their realms) attempted to create a fixed capital to rival that of Byzantium, an ancient culture legendary for its beauty and wealth.

A closer look at Charlemagne
The major record of Charlemagne's personal

Generation 1 (cont.)

achievements is the Vita Caroli Magni, the first medieval biography. Written by Einhard between 817 and 836, this biography is largely a firsthand account, as Einhard was a member of the palace school during Charlemagne's reign and was his close associate.

In the Vita is the actual physical description of the man who has since become one of the greatest legendary heroes of the Middle Ages (476-1453 C. E.). Toward his friends Charlemagne was lighthearted, and he particularly enjoyed the company of others. Yet toward his enemies he was often a cruel warrior feared for his strength and ability. Although primarily a man of action, he had great admiration for learning and spoke Latin fluently. He studied Greek and the liberal arts and thus combined, to some extent, the personality of a warrior and a scholar.

Charlemagne's administration
What is most striking about Charlemagne's rule was that he was able to maintain, largely through the strength of his own personality, a centralized state wherein royal authority came first. Charlemagne also maintained a small group of the best warriors, the vassi dominici, who helped him enforce his authority. During the course of his reign Charlemagne sent a number of written instructions to his officials. These enactments, known as the Capitularii had the force of law and

were executed directly by the royal agents. They are extremely valuable as sources in understanding the social and legal structure of Carolingian France.

In general, Charlemagne's reign was a period of internal calm and prosperity because of his military and political ability. He succeeded, through diplomatic negotiations, in having his imperial title recognized by the Byzantine emperor. Through his program of cultural revival and changes to the Church, he succeeded in improving the level of civilization in the West.

Carolingian culture
Charlemagne's support of the arts and letters had several purposes beyond the general improvement of culture and literacy in the empire. One of the major purposes was to provide an educated clergy (a group of religious servants) that could undertake many of the administrative tasks of government. A second purpose was to win the acceptance of orthodox doctrine, or rules of the church, as well as a uniform religious practice throughout the empire. Such uniformity not only strengthened the Church but also centralized the administration of the empire. Still, a third purpose of this cultural revival was to improve the status and authority of Charlemagne himself, who thus appeared as the defender and protector of the Church, of orthodoxy, and of education.

Generation 1 (cont.)

The intellectual traditions and educational institutions supported by Charlemagne greatly influenced the development of Western culture. Charlemagne expanded the number of schools, and the quality of education was greatly improved.

His last years
In 806, at the age of sixty-four, Charlemagne took measures to provide for the succession of his empire. He divided the realm among his three sons-Charles, Pepin, and Louis. But the death of Charles in April 810 was soon followed by that of Pepin. The remaining son, Louis, later called "the Pious," the least warlike and aggressive of the three, was left as the sole heir to the empire. He was crowned by his father in 813.

The last years of Charlemagne's reign saw difficult times. Civil disorder increased as did disease and famine (drastic food shortages). Additionally, there were troubles on the frontiers. In many respects, the future looked dark. In 811 Charlemagne made his final will, giving a more sizable portion of his treasures to various churches of the realm than to his own heirs. He died on January 28, 814, and was buried at his palace at Aachen.

For More Information
Bullough, Donald. The Age of Charlemagne. 2nd ed. New York: Exeter Books, 1980.

Generation 1 (cont.)

Collins, Roger. Charlemagne. Toronto: University of Toronto Press, 1998.

Lamb, Harold. Charlemagne: The Legend and the Man. Garden City, NY: Doubleday, 1954.

Riché, Pierre. Daily Life in the World of Charlemagne. Philadelphia, PA: University of Pennsylvania Press, 1978.

Charlemagne and Hildegarde had the following child:

2. i. LOUIS I[2] was born in Aug 778 AD in Gargonne. He died on 20 Jun 840 AD in Mainz, Mainz, Rhineland-Palatinate, Germany. He married Judith of Bavaria, daughter of Guelph I and Edith, in Feb 819 AD. She died on 19 Apr 843 AD.

Generation 2

2. **LOUIS I**[2] (Charlemagne[1]) was born in Aug 778 AD in Gargonne. He died on 20 Jun 840 AD in Mainz, Mainz, Rhineland-Palatinate, Germany. He married Judith of Bavaria, daughter of Guelph I and Edith, in Feb 819 AD. She died on 19 Apr 843 AD.

Generation 2 (cont.)

Notes for Louis I:
le Debonnaire, King of the Franks, Emperor of the West 814-840.

Louis I and Judith of Bavaria had the following child:

3. i. CHARLES II[3] was born on 13 Jun 828 AD in Frankfort-on-Main. He died on 06 Oct 877 AD in Mt. Cenis in the Alps. He married Errmentrude, daughter of Odo and Engeltrude, in Dec 842 AD. She died on 06 Oct 869 AD.

Generation 3

3. **CHARLES II**[3] (Louis I[2], Charlemagne[1]) was born on 13 Jun 828 AD in Frankfort-on-Main. He died on 06 Oct 877 AD in Mt. Cenis in the Alps. He married Errmentrude, daughter of Odo and Engeltrude, in Dec 842 AD. She died on 06 Oct 869 AD.

Notes for Charles II:
The Bald, King of the Franks, 840-877, Emperor from 25 December 875-877.

Charles II and Errmentrude had the following child:

4. i. LOUIS II[4] was born in 844 AD. He died on 10 Apr 879 AD in Compeigne. He married Adelaide of

Generation 3 (cont.)

Paris in 868 AD. She died after 901 AD.

Generation 4

4. **Louis II**[4] (Charles II[3], Louis I[2], Charlemagne[1]) was born in 844 AD. He died on 10 Apr 879 AD in Compeigne. He married Adelaide of Paris in 868 AD. She died after 901 AD.

Notes for Louis II:
The Stammer, King of the Franks 877-879, Emperor 878-879.

Louis II and Adelaide of Paris had the following child:

5. i. Charles III[5]. He married Elgiva Edgina, daughter of Edward the Elder and Edgiva, in 919 AD. She died in 951 AD.

Generation 5

5. **Charles III**[5] (Louis II[4], Charles II[3], Louis I[2], Charlemagne[1]). He married Elgiva Edgina, daughter of Edward the Elder and Edgiva, in 919 AD. She died in 951 AD.

Notes for Charles III:
The Simple.

Charles III and Elgiva Edgina had the following child:

Generation 5 (cont.)

6. i. LOUIS IV^6 was born in 921 AD. He died on 10 Sep 954 AD. He married GERBERGA. She died on 05 May 984 AD.

Generation 6

6. **LOUIS IV**^{6} (Charles III^5, Louis II^4, Charles II^3, Louis I^2, Charlemagne^1) was born in 921 AD. He died on 10 Sep 954 AD. He married **GERBERGA**. She died on 05 May 984 AD.

Notes for Louis IV:
D'Outre-mer, King of France 936-954.

Notes for Gerberga:
The daughter of Henry I, German Emperor, by Matilda, daughter of Dietrich of Westphalia.

Louis IV and Gerberga had the following child:

7. i. ALBERT I^7 was born about 920 AD. He died in 988 AD.

Generation 7

7. **ALBERT I**^{7} (Louis IV^6, Charles III^5, Louis II^4, Charles II^3, Louis I^2, Charlemagne^1) was born about 920 AD. He died in 988 AD.

Notes for Albert I:
The Pious, Count of Vermandios.

Albert I had the following child:

8. i. HERBERT II^8. He married GERBERGA.

Descendants of Charlemagne

Generation 8

8. **HERBERT II**^{8} (Albert I^{7}, Louis IV^{6}, Charles III^{5}, Louis II^{4}, Charles II^{3}, Louis I^{2}, Charlemagne^{1}). He married **GERBERGA**.

Notes for Herbert II:
Count of Vermandios and Troyes.

Herbert II and Gerberga had the following child:

9. i. HERBERT III^{9} was born in 955 AD. He died about 1000. He married ERMENGARDE.

Generation 9

9. **HERBERT III**^{9} (Herbert II^{8}, Albert I^{7}, Louis IV^{6}, Charles III^{5}, Louis II^{4}, Charles II^{3}, Louis I^{2}, Charlemagne^{1}) was born in 955 AD. He died about 1000. He married **ERMENGARDE**.

Herbert III and Ermengarde had the following child:

10. i. PA(R)VIE^{10}. She married OTTO. He was born about 1000. He died on 25 May 1045.

Generation 10

10. **PA(R)VIE**^{10} (Herbert III^{9}, Herbert II^{8}, Albert I^{7}, Louis IV^{6}, Charles III^{5}, Louis II^{4}, Charles II^{3}, Louis I^{2}, Charlemagne^{1}). She married **OTTO**. He was born about 1000. He died on 25 May 1045.

Notes for Otto:
Count De Vermandois; married Pa(r)vie.

Generation 10 (cont.)

Otto and Pa(r)vie had the following child:

11. i. HERBERT IV[11] was born about 1032. He died about 1080. He married ADELA DE VEXIN.

Generation 11

11. **HERBERT IV**[11] (Pa(r)vie[10], Herbert III[9], Herbert II[8], Albert I[7], Louis IV[6], Charles III[5], Louis II[4], Charles II[3], Louis I[2], Charlemagne[1]) was born about 1032. He died about 1080. He married **ADELA DE VEXIN**.

Notes for Herbert IV:
Count De Varmandios and Valois.

Herbert IV and Adela De Vexin had the following child:

12. i. ADELAIDE[12] ADELHEID. She died about 1120. She married HENRY MAGNUS. He died in 1101.

Generation 12

12. **ADELAIDE**[12] **ADELHEID** (Herbert IV[11], Pa(r)vie[10], Herbert III[9], Herbert II[8], Albert I[7], Louis IV[6], Charles III[5], Louis II[4], Charles II[3], Louis I[2], Charlemagne[1], Herbert IV[11], Otto). She died about 1120. She married **HENRY MAGNUS**. He died in 1101.

Notes for Henry Magnus:
Duke of France and Burgundy, Leader of the First Crusade, Marquis of Orleans, Count of Amiens,

Generation 12 (cont.)

Chaumont, Paris, Valois, Vermandois, etc. Son of Henry I, King of France, by Anne, daughter of Yaroslav of Kiev.

Henry Magnus and Adelaide Adelheid had the following child:

i. ISABEL[13] DE VERMANDOIS. She died on 13 Feb 1131. She married William De Warenne in 1119.

Notes for Isabel De Vermandois: Countess of Leicester.

Notes for William De Warenne: Second Earl of Surrey, who died 11 May 1138.

Descendants of William De Warenne

Generation 1

1. **William[1] De Warenne** . He married (1) **Gundred**. He married (2) **Isabel De Vermandois**, daughter of Henry Magnus and Adelaide Adelheid, in 1119. She died on 13 Feb 1131.

   Notes for William De Warenne:
   Second Earl of Surrey, who died 11 May 1138.

   William De Warenne and Gundred had the following child:

   2. i. Ada[2] De Warenne. She died in 1178. She married Henry Huntington in 1139. He was born in 1114. He died on 12 Jun 1152.

   Notes for Isabel De Vermandois:
   Countess of Leicester.

Generation 2

2. **Ada[2] De Warenne** (William[1]). She died in 1178. She married Henry Huntington in 1139. He was born in 1114. He died on 12 Jun 1152.

   Henry Huntington and Ada De Warenne had the following child:

   3. i. David Earl Of[3] Huntington. He married Maud on 26 Aug 1190. She was born in 1171. She died in 1233.

Generation 3

3. **David Earl Of[3] Huntington** (Ada[2] De Warenne, William[1] De Warenne, Henry). He married Maud on 26 Aug 1190. She was born in 1171. She died in

Generation 3 (cont.)

1233.

Notes for David Earl of Huntington:
One of the most accomplished princes of his time.

David Earl of Huntington and Maud had the following child:

4. i. ISABEL[4]. She married ROBERT DE BRUS.

Generation 4

4. **ISABEL**[4] (David Earl of[3] Huntington, Ada[2] De Warenne, William[1] De Warenne, David Earl of[3] Huntington, Henry Huntington). She married **ROBERT DE BRUS**.

Notes for Isabel:
Isabel of Huntington, daughter of David, Earl of Huntington and Maud.

Notes for Robert De Brus:
6th Lord of Annandale, was born in 1226 and died at Lochmaben Castle 31 March 1295. He married in May 1240 Isabel de Clare, born 2 November 1226 and died after 10 July 1264. He was a Crusader and a claimant of the Crown of Scotland. She was the second daughter of Gilbert, Earl de Clare, 7th Earl of Hertford and Glouester, a Magna Charta Surety, who married Isabel Marshall on 9 October 1217. He was born ca. 1180 and died at Penros, Brittany, 25 October 1230.

Robert De Brus and Isabel had the following child:

5. i. ROBERT[5] DE BRUS. He married MARGARET.

Generation 5

5. **Robert[5] De Brus** (Isabel[4], David Earl of[3] Huntington, Ada[2] De Warenne, William[1] De Warenne, Robert). He married **Margaret**.

Notes for Robert De Brus:
7th Lord of Annandale, was born in July 1243 and died before 4 April 1304. In 1271, he married Margaret (Marjorie) Countess of Carrick, who died 27 October 1292, daughter of Nigel, Earl of Carrick, and Margaret, daughter of Walter, Steward of Scotland. Magna Charta Surety.

Robert De Brus and Margaret had the following child:

6. i. The Bruce[6] Robert. He married Isabel.

Generation 6

6. **The Bruce[6] Robert** (Robert[5] De Brus, Isabel[4], David Earl of[3] Huntington, Ada[2] De Warenne, William[1] De Warenne, Robert[5] De Brus, Robert De Brus). He married **Isabel**.

Notes for The Bruce Robert:
King of Scots, born at Writtle, County Essex, on 11 July 1274 and died a Cadross, Scotland 7 June 1329. He married 1295 Isabel, who died in 1297, daughter of Donald, Earl of Mar, by his first wife Helen, daughter of Llewellyn, Prince of North Wales.

The Bruce Robert and Isabel had the following child:

7. i. Marjory[7] Bruce. She married Walter Stuart Stewart.

Generation 7

Generation 7 (cont.)

7. **MARJORY[7] BRUCE** (The Bruce[6] Robert, Robert[5] De Brus, Isabel[4], David Earl of[3] Huntington, Ada[2] De Warenne, William[1] De Warenne, The Bruce[6] Robert, Robert[5] De Brus, Robert De Brus). She married **WALTER STUART STEWART**.

Notes for Marjory Bruce:
Born before 1297 and died 2 March 1315/16. She married in 1315 Walter Stuart (Stewart), Lord High Steward of Scotland, born 1292 and died 9 April 1329. He is buried at Paisley, Scotland. He was the son of James Stewart (died 9 April 1309) and Cecilia, daughter of Patrick, Earl of Dunbar.

Walter Stuart Stewart and Marjory Bruce had the following child:

8. i. STUART ROBERT[8] II.

Generation 8

8. **STUART ROBERT[8] II** (Marjory[7] Bruce, The Bruce[6] Robert, Robert[5] De Brus, Isabel[4], David Earl of[3] Huntington, Ada[2] De Warenne, William[1] De Warenne, Walter Stuart Stewart).

Notes for Stuart Robert II:
King of Scots, was born 21 March 1315/16 and died 19 April 1390 at Dundonald Castle. He was Earl of Atholt, Earl of Strathern, and King of Scotland. He married, second, Euphemia, daughter of Hugh, Earl of Ross, and the widow of John Randolph, Earl of Moray, dispensation 2 May 1355.

Stuart Robert II had the following child:

Generation 8 (cont.)

9. i. CATHERINE[9] STEWART. She married DAVID LINDSAY.

Generation 9

9. **CATHERINE[9] STEWART** (Stuart Robert[8] II, Marjory[7] Bruce, The Bruce[6] Robert, Robert[5] De Brus, Isabel[4], David Earl of[3] Huntington, Ada[2] De Warenne, William[1] De Warenne, Stuart Robert[8] II, Walter Stuart Stewart). She married **DAVID LINDSAY**.

Notes for David Lindsay:
1st Earl of Crawford, created Earl on 21 April 1398. He was Admiral of Scotland in 1403 and Ambassador to England in 1405. Born ca. 1360, died in February 1406/07.

LINDSAY/LINDSEY
INTRODUCTION
The descent from Niord, King of Sweden (40 B.C.), deduced from the Danish and Swedish Archives, has been fully compiled by Harrison, historian of the West Riding of York. According to William Harrison in his History of York, Chart I, "Niord is descended from Odin, King of Arcadia (761 B.C.) who came out of Scythia with an army of Goths, conquered Northern Europe, settled Sweden, lived and died there. Odin was forty-first in descent from Eric, King of the Goths in Scandinavia, living in the time of Serene, great-grandfather of Abraham." There are 60 generations from Niord to 1976. (The Ancient Swedish Line). The Lindsay lineage goes back 42 generations through the Scottish Kings Robert Bruce and Malcolm III (who defeated Macbeth) to Eugenius VII who was elected King of Scotland in 70 A.D.

Generation 9 (cont.)

(Lineage to the Kings of Scotland)
There are at least two Sureties for Magna Charta in the Lindsay line: Gilbert, Earl of Clare, 7th Earl of Hertford and Gloucester, whose daughter married Robert Bruce. Gilbert's father, Richard, 6th Earl of Clare was born before 1182 and died in 1230. He was Lord of Hardleur and Montrevillers in 1202, Earl of Hertford and Clare in 1217 and Earl of Gloucester in 1217. He is buried at Tewkesbury. His father, Richard de Clare, was born before 1162 and died in 1217. He was the third Earl of Hertford in 1173, Earl of Clare in 1173 and Envoy from the Barons to King John 9 November 1215. He is buried at Tonbridge. His arms: Or, Chevrons Gules to which his son Gilbert added a Label of three points for a difference.
(The Magna Charta Lineage)
Early Scottish Charters bear witness to the name de Lindesis back as early as 1116, a name which evolved through common usage to become Lindsay under the convention of Scottish surnames. The Lindsay family has played a significant role in Scotland's history as far back as the reign of David I. Their exploit, contributions and achievements have been well documented in historical accounts and in public records.
Gilbert de Ghent accompanied Duke William in his conquest of England and for his services was given extensive lands near Lincoln and in the surrounding Lindsey area. He also became known as Gilbert de Lindsey by virtue of the land he obtained and this was the name carried by his offspring, Walter and William, when they settled in the Borders of Scotland. In accordance to the convention of Scottish surnames this de Lindsey generally evolved into the surname

Lindsey, in its most common use.
The early arrival of de Lindsays to Scotland is shrouded in a mist of speculation. When the de Lindsays arrived to Scotland, they took lands at Ericildon in Roxburghshire, now known as Earlston, on the banks of the Leader Water.
Gilbert de Ghent was born about 1048. He took part in the Norman invasion of 1066 with the strong contingent of Flemish supporters of William the Conqueror. His son Walter, born ca. 1080, came to be known as Sir Walter de Lindsay. Sir Walter reportedly accompanied David, Earl of Huntington (who became King David I) when he came north to the Lowlands in the early 1100s.
A geographical representation of the migration north is shown in the map from the Norman invasion of 1066 up until the time where the main branch of the family established themselves in Glenesk, Angus around 1358 following the marriage of Sir Alexander Lindsay to Catherine Stirling, daughter of Sir John Stirling of Edzell.
The three sons of William de Lindsay of Earlston established three main family branches of Luffness, Crawford and Lamberton around 1200. The family tree shows the development of the Lindsay family branches from Charlemagne to Balcarres. This Lindsay/Lindsey family stems from the Crawford branch which terminated when Sir Gerald de Lindsay died in 1249 leaving the estate to his sister Alice de Lindsay, wife of Sir Henry Pinkeney. However, the title Crawford was retrieved by the Scottish authorities who bestowed it on Bruce's staunch supporter, Sir Alexander of Luffness, the heir male of the Scottish Lindsays. (Lord Lindsay, Lives of the Lindsays: A

Memoir of the Houses of Crawford and Balcarres, vol. 1 [John Murray, London, Second Edition 1858], pp. 117-118).
The Lindsays of Crawford originally built a fortified tower close to the village of Crawford, near Abington, named Tower Lindsay which became a more substantial fortification, Crawford Castle. It commanded a strategic position built on a hill overlooking the west coast route to Scotland near to the river crossing the Clyde. The ruins of the castle can be seen today, standing on the knoll surrounded by a thicket of trees. The Lindsays' of Crawford were strong supporters of Scottish independence. Sir Alexander Lindsay, who was very close to Bruce and Wallace, was a marked man on Edward I's wanted list and took part in many of the conflicts during the Wars of Independence. He served in the Scottish Parliament until at least 309.

David Lindsay and Catherine Stewart had the following child:

10. i. ALEXANDER[10] LINDSAY was born in 1387. He married MARIETTA DUNBAR.

Generation 10

10. **ALEXANDER[10] LINDSAY** (Catherine[9] Stewart, Stuart Robert[8] II, Marjory[7] Bruce, The Bruce[6] Robert, Robert[5] De Brus, Isabel[4], David Earl of[3] Huntington, Ada[2] De Warenne, William[1] De Warenne) was born in 1387. He married **MARIETTA DUNBAR**.

Generation 10 (cont.)

Notes for Alexander Lindsay:
2nd Earl of Crawford, born ca. 1387, was knighted 21 May 1424, and died after 31 March 1438. He was Ambassador to England 1429-1430.

Alexander Lindsay and Marietta Dunbar had the following child:

11. i. DAVID[11] LINDSAY. He married KATHERINE STEWART.

Generation 11

11. **DAVID[11] LINDSAY** (Alexander[10], Catherine[9] Stewart, Stuart Robert[8] II, Marjory[7] Bruce, The Bruce[6] Robert, Robert[5] De Brus, Isabel[4], David Earl of[3] Huntington, Ada[2] De Warenne, William[1] De Warenne, Alexander[10], David). He married **KATHERINE STEWART**.

David Lindsay and Katherine Stewart had the following children:

12. i. DAVID[12] LINDSAY was born in 1410 in Crawford, Lanarkshire, Scotland. He died on 17 Jan 1446 in Angusshire, Scotland, Battle of Aberbrothock.. He married MARGORIE OGILVIE. She was born in 1410. She died in 1476.

13. ii. ALEXANDER LINDSAY. He died in 1439. He married CATHERINE STIRLING.

Generation 12

12. **DAVID[12] LINDSAY** (David[11], Alexander[10], Catherine[9] Stewart, Stuart Robert[8] II, Marjory[7] Bruce, The Bruce[6] Robert, Robert[5] De Brus, Isabel[4], David Earl of[3]

Huntington, Ada[2] De Warenne, William[1] De Warenne) was born in 1410 in Crawford, Lanarkshire, Scotland. He died on 17 Jan 1446 in Angusshire, Scotland, Battle of Aberbrothock.. He married **MARGORIE OGILVIE**. She was born in 1410. She died in 1476.

Notes for David Lindsay:
Lord, 3rd Earl of Crawford. Sheriff of Aberdeen, died in Battle of Aberbrothock 7 January 1445/46.

David Lindsay and Margorie Ogilvie had the following child:

14. i. WALTER[13] LINDSAY was born in 1445 in Auchtermuchty, Fife, Scotland. He died in 1517 in Finhaven Castle, Angusshire, Scotland. He married (1) ISABEL LIVINGSTON. She was born in 1432. She died on 15 Jun 1509 in Perth, Perthshire, Scotland. He married (2) JEAN JANET JEANETTE SINCLAIR/ST. CLAIR. He married (3) SOPHIA LIVINGSTON.

13. **ALEXANDER[12] LINDSAY** (David[11], Alexander[10], Catherine[9] Stewart, Stuart Robert[8] II, Marjory[7] Bruce, The Bruce[6] Robert, Robert[5] De Brus, Isabel[4], David Earl of[3] Huntington, Ada[2] De Warenne, William[1] De Warenne, David[11], Alexander[10], David). He died in 1439. He married **CATHERINE STIRLING**.

Notes for Alexander Lindsay:
Sir knighted at the cornation of King James May 21, 1424, Lord, 1st Earl of Crawford. A Genealogical and Heritage History of the Peerage and Baronetage.

Generation 12 (cont.)

Acquired lands at Edzell and Glenesk through marriage to Catherine Stirling in 1358.

Notes for Catherine Stirling:
The Stirlings of Glenesk are said to have been descendants of Henry de Strevelin, youngest son of David, Earl of Huntington, the brother of King William, the Lion. The Stirlings acquired Glenesk at a very early date and the last male proprietor of the name was Sir John de Striveling, whose daughter and heiress, married in 1365, Sir Alexander Lindsay, third son of Sir David Lindsay of Crawford. Sir David Lindsay, who was created Earl of Crawford in 1398, was the eldest child of Sir Alexander Lindsay and Catherine Stirling. Lord Lindsay says that "The cognisance of the Stirlins of Glenesk as three stars, in common with the house of De Moravia and othern northern families (*Lives of the Lindsays,* Vol. I, p. 51) (the Stirlings being even sometimes being territorially De Movaria . . . By way of a family differences, in right of his descent from Ctherine de Striveline, mother of David, first Earl of Crawford, the daughter and heiress of Sir Joh Striveline of Glenesk (head of an ancient and powerful family, whose arms consiste solely of stars), he added the stars to his Coat. The stars are still visibly sculptured upon the prominent parts of the old Castle of Edzell, which lay within the barony of Glenesk. Hence by Scottish practice, they became what were termed the 'feudal arms' of the Barony, which were also derived from the first tenants in capite or possession--in this stance, undoubtedly the Strivelynes."

Tradition gives another account of the succession of

the Lindsays to Glenesk. It is said that the last Sir John Striveline of Glenesk had a son and a daughter. "They were left orphans and the former, small of stature and greatly deformed in body as familiarily known by the diminitive cognomen of 'Jackie Stirlin.' Although physically defective, he enjoyed excellent health and was neither impervious to the softer feelings of humanity nor too unseemly for the kindly eyes of women, by one of whom, the lovely daughter of a neighboring baron, his offer of marriage was accepted.

"This was altogether contrary to the wishes and expectations of his sister and her lover, the gallant Sir Alexander Lindsay, and all remonstrances having failed to prevent the nuptials, they laid a deep and heartless scheme for his overthrow, and one evening while taking an airing alone in the wooded defile, he was pounced upon by a masked assailant and summarily dispatchd at a point still pointed out a little to the north of the Castle." (*Land of the Lindsays, p. 26)*.

Part of the old Castle of Edzell, once the residence of the Stirlings of Glenesk, is called "Stirling Tower" and is believed to have been erected by them.

Alexander Lindsay and Catherine Stirling had the following child:

12. i. DAVID[12] LINDSAY was born in 1410 in Crawford, Lanarkshire, Scotland. He died on 17 Jan 1446 in Angusshire, Scotland, Battle of Aberbrothock.. He married MARGORIE OGILVIE. She was

born in 1410. She died in 1476.

Generation 13

14. **WALTER**[13] **LINDSAY** (David[12], David[11], Alexander[10], Catherine[9] Stewart, Stuart Robert[8] II, Marjory[7] Bruce, The Bruce[6] Robert, Robert[5] De Brus, Isabel[4], David Earl of[3] Huntington, Ada[2] De Warenne, William[1] De Warenne) was born in 1445 in Auchtermuchty, Fife, Scotland. He died in 1517 in Finhaven Castle, Angusshire, Scotland. He married (1) **ISABEL LIVINGSTON**. She was born in 1432. She died on 15 Jun 1509 in Perth, Perthshire, Scotland. He married (2) **JEAN JANET JEANETTE SINCLAIR/ST. CLAIR**. He married (3) **SOPHIA LIVINGSTON**.

Notes for Walter Lindsay:
Married in 1470, died 1475. See "Wood's Douglas's Peerage of Scotland, " I, 164, 376. "Tutor" to Earl David. Earl of Crawford. Third son of Alexander 2nd Earl of Crawford. Magna Charta Barons and their American Descendants; the Descent of General Robert Edward Lee from Robert The Bruce, of Scotland.

Notes for Isabel Livingston:
Also name given as Sophia.

Walter Lindsay and Isabel Livingston had the following child:

15. i. DAVID[14] LINDSAY was born in 1455 in Edzell, Aberdeenshire, Scotland. He died on 27 Nov 1528 in Auchtermonzie, Scotland. He married (1) ELIZABETH SPENCE. She died in 1532. He married (2) AGNES OGILVY.

Generation 13 (cont.)

He married (3) KATHERINE FOTHERINGTON. She was born in 1460. She died in 1488 in Somme, Picardie, France.

Walter Lindsay and Jean Janet Jeanette Sinclair/St. Clair had the following children:

ii. ELISABETH LINDSAY was born in 1505.

iii. SIBILLA LINDSAY was born in 1515.

iv. ISOBEL LINDSAY was born in 1526.

v. DAVID LINDSAY was born in 1527.

vi. ELIZABETH ALEXANDER LINDSAY was born in 1531.

Generation 14

15. **DAVID**[14] **LINDSAY** (Walter[13], David[12], David[11], Alexander[10], Catherine[9] Stewart, Stuart Robert[8] II, Marjory[7] Bruce, The Bruce[6] Robert, Robert[5] De Brus, Isabel[4], David Earl of[3] Huntington, Ada[2] De Warenne, William[1] De Warenne) was born in 1455 in Edzell, Aberdeenshire, Scotland. He died on 27 Nov 1528 in Auchtermonzie, Scotland. He married (1) **ELIZABETH SPENCE**. She died in 1532. He married (2) **AGNES OGILVY**. He married (3) **KATHERINE FOTHERINGTON**. She was born in 1460. She died in 1488 in Somme, Picardie, France.

Notes for David Lindsay:
Sir David Lindsay, of Beaufort and Edzell, a Member of Parliment, 1487, died in 1528. He married first, Katherine, daughter of Thomas Fotheringham of Powrie. The Lindsays were prominent in both

England and Scotland from the late 11th century.

David Lindsay and Elizabeth Spence had the following child:

16. i. WALTER THOMAS[15] LINDSAY was born in 1480 in Edzell, Angus, Scotland. He died on 09 Sep 1513 in Battle of Flodden Field, Branxton, Northumberland, England. He married Elizabeth Erskine in 1500 in Edzell, Lanarkshire, Scotland. She was born in 1475 in Edzell, Angus, Scotland. She died in 1540 in Haddington, East Lothian, Scotland.

David Lindsay and Agnes Ogilvy had the following child:

16. i. WALTER THOMAS[15] LINDSAY was born in 1480 in Edzell, Angus, Scotland. He died on 09 Sep 1513 in Battle of Flodden Field, Branxton, Northumberland, England. He married Elizabeth Erskine in 1500 in Edzell, Lanarkshire, Scotland. She was born in 1475 in Edzell, Angus, Scotland. She died in 1540 in Haddington, East Lothian, Scotland.

David Lindsay and Katherine Fotherington had the following children:

17. iii. RACHEL LINDSAY was born in 1563. She died on 02 Dec 1639 in Ross, Scotland. She married JOHN SPOTTISWOODE. He was born in 1565.

Generation 14 (cont.)

He died on 17 Nov 1639 in London, England.

18. iv. Walter Lindsay. He died on 09 Sep 1513. He married Erskine.

v. Alexander Lindsay.

vi. David Lindsay.

Generation 15

16. **Walter Thomas[15] Lindsay** (David[14], Walter[13], David[12], David[11], Alexander[10], Catherine[9] Stewart, Stuart Robert[8] II, Marjory[7] Bruce, The Bruce[6] Robert, Robert[5] De Brus, Isabel[4], David Earl of[3] Huntington, Ada[2] De Warenne, William[1] De Warenne) was born in 1480 in Edzell, Angus, Scotland. He died on 09 Sep 1513 in Battle of Flodden Field, Branxton, Northumberland, England. He married Elizabeth Erskine in 1500 in Edzell, Lanarkshire, Scotland. She was born in 1475 in Edzell, Angus, Scotland. She died in 1540 in Haddington, East Lothian, Scotland.

Walter Thomas Lindsay and Elizabeth Erskine had the following children:

i. Bishop[16] Lindsay was born in 1505.

19. ii. Alexander David Lindsay was born in 1508. He married (1) Janet Gray. He married (2) Catherine (Calder) Campbell.

20. iii. Robert Lindsay was born in 1509.

21. iv. Alexander David Lindsay was born in 1532 in Pittormie, Scotland. He married Rachel (Mathers) Barclay.

Generation 15 (cont.)

22. v. JOHN LINDSAY. He married JOAN STEWART.

17. **RACHEL LINDSAY** (David[14], Walter[13], David[12], David[11], Alexander[10], Catherine[9] Stewart, Stuart Robert[8] II, Marjory[7] Bruce, The Bruce[6] Robert, Robert[5] De Brus, Isabel[4], David Earl of[3] Huntington, Ada[2] De Warenne, William[1] De Warenne) was born in 1563. She died on 02 Dec 1639 in Ross, Scotland. She married **JOHN SPOTTISWOODE**. He was born in 1565. He died on 17 Nov 1639 in London, England.

Notes for John Spottiswoode:
Archbishop of St. Andrews in 1615; Lord High Chancellor of Scotland, 1635. He crowned King Charles I, at Holyrood, in 1639. Buried by King's demand at Westminster Abbey (see Playfair's "British Family Antiquity," VIII, 805.

John Spottiswoode and Rachel Lindsay had the following child:

23. i. ROBERT SPOTTISWOODE was born in 1596 in Dunipace, Stirlingshire, Scotland. He died on 16 Jan 1646 in St. Andrews, Fife, Scotland. He married Bethia Morrison, daughter of Alexander Morrison and Eleanor Maule, in 1629. She was born in 1608. She died on 17 Nov 1639 in Wedderburn Castle, Berwickshire, Scotland.

18. **WALTER[15] LINDSAY** (David[14], Walter[13], David[12], David[11], Alexander[10], Catherine[9] Stewart, Stuart Robert[8] II, Marjory[7] Bruce, The Bruce[6] Robert, Robert[5] De Brus, Isabel[4], David Earl of[3] Huntington,

Generation 15 (cont.)

Ada[2] De Warenne, William[1] De Warenne, David[14], Walter[13], David[12], David[11], Alexander[10], David). He died on 09 Sep 1513. He married **ERSKINE**.

Notes for Erskine:
"The Younger" of Edzell, was killed at the Battle of Flodden Field 9 September 1513.

Walter Lindsay and Erskine had the following children:

20. i. ROBERT[16] LINDSAY was born in 1509.

21. ii. ALEXANDER DAVID LINDSAY was born in 1532 in Pittormie, Scotland. He married RACHEL (MATHERS) BARCLAY.

22. iii. JOHN LINDSAY. He married JOAN STEWART.

Generation 16

19. **ALEXANDER DAVID[16] LINDSAY** (Walter Thomas[15], David[14], Walter[13], David[12], David[11], Alexander[10], Catherine[9] Stewart, Stuart Robert[8] II, Marjory[7] Bruce, The Bruce[6] Robert, Robert[5] De Brus, Isabel[4], David Earl of[3] Huntington, Ada[2] De Warenne, William[1] De Warenne) was born in 1508. He married (1) **JANET GRAY**. He married (2) **CATHERINE (CALDER) CAMPBELL**.

Alexander David Lindsay and Catherine (Calder) Campbell had the following children:

24. i. DAVID ROSS[17] LINDSAY was born in 1532 in Pittormie. He died in 1613 in Leith, Edinburgh, Scotland. He married (1) JONETA RAMSAY. He married (2) HELEN HARRESON.

ii. DAVID LINDSAY.

Generation 16 (cont.)

iii. JOHN LINDSAY.

20. **ROBERT[16] LINDSAY** (Walter Thomas[15], David[14], Walter[13], David[12], David[11], Alexander[10], Catherine[9] Stewart, Stuart Robert[8] II, Marjory[7] Bruce, The Bruce[6] Robert, Robert[5] De Brus, Isabel[4], David Earl of[3] Huntington, Ada[2] De Warenne, William[1] De Warenne) was born in 1509.

Robert Lindsay had the following child:

25. i. DAVID[17] LINDSAY was born in 1531 in Halftoun, Puttorlie, Scotland. He died on 17 Dec 1613 in Annatland, Angusshire, Scotland.

21. **ALEXANDER DAVID[16] LINDSAY** (Walter Thomas[15], David[14], Walter[13], David[12], David[11], Alexander[10], Catherine[9] Stewart, Stuart Robert[8] II, Marjory[7] Bruce, The Bruce[6] Robert, Robert[5] De Brus, Isabel[4], David Earl of[3] Huntington, Ada[2] De Warenne, William[1] De Warenne) was born in 1532 in Pittormie, Scotland. He married **RACHEL (MATHERS) BARCLAY**.

Alexander David Lindsay and Rachel (Mathers) Barclay had the following children:

24. i. DAVID ROSS[17] LINDSAY was born in 1532 in Pittormie. He died in 1613 in Leith, Edinburgh, Scotland. He married (1) JONETA RAMSAY. He married (2) HELEN HARRESON.

ii. DAVID LINDSAY.

iii. JOHN LINDSAY.

22. **JOHN[16] LINDSAY** (Walter Thomas[15], David[14], Walter[13], David[12], David[11], Alexander[10], Catherine[9] Stewart,

Generation 16 (cont.)

Stuart Robert[8] II, Marjory[7] Bruce, The Bruce[6] Robert, Robert[5] De Brus, Isabel[4], David Earl of[3] Huntington, Ada[2] De Warenne, William[1] De Warenne, Walter[15], David[14], Walter[13], David[12], David[11], Alexander[10], David). He married **JOAN STEWART**.

John Lindsay and Joan Stewart had the following children:

26. i. PATRICK[17] LINDSAY was born in 1526. He married ISABELLA PITCAIRN.

ii. JOHN LINDSAY. He died in 1563.

Notes for John Lindsay:
5th Lord Lindsay of the Byres (died 1563) was a Scottish judge.

23. **ROBERT SPOTTISWOODE** (Rachel Lindsay, David[14] Lindsay, Walter[13] Lindsay, David[12] Lindsay, David[11] Lindsay, Alexander[10] Lindsay, Catherine[9] Stewart, Stuart Robert[8] II, Marjory[7] Bruce, The Bruce[6] Robert, Robert[5] De Brus, Isabel[4], David Earl of[3] Huntington, Ada[2] De Warenne, William[1] De Warenne) was born in 1596 in Dunipace, Stirlingshire, Scotland. He died on 16 Jan 1646 in St. Andrews, Fife, Scotland. He married Bethia Morrison, daughter of Alexander Morrison and Eleanor Maule, in 1629. She was born in 1608. She died on 17 Nov 1639 in Wedderburn Castle, Berwickshire, Scotland.

Notes for Robert Spottiswoode:
See the "Sottiswood Miscellany," 1844, Vol. I. He was a member of the Privy Council to James VI, of Scotland and was appointed by King Charles I. Lawyer, Knighted Sir, Beheaded, January 16, 1646.

Generation 16 (cont.)

Robert Spottiswoode and Bethia Morrison had the following child:

i. ROBERT SPOTTISWOODE was born in 1637. He died in 1680.

Notes for Robert Spottiswoode:
Genealogy of the Spotswood Family in Scotland and Virginia.

Generation 17

24. **DAVID ROSS**[17] **LINDSAY** (Alexander David[16], Walter Thomas[15], David[14], Walter[13], David[12], David[11], Alexander[10], Catherine[9] Stewart, Stuart Robert[8] II, Marjory[7] Bruce, The Bruce[6] Robert, Robert[5] De Brus, Isabel[4], David Earl of[3] Huntington, Ada[2] De Warenne, William[1] De Warenne) was born in 1532 in Pittormie. He died in 1613 in Leith, Edinburgh, Scotland. He married (1) **JONETA RAMSAY**. He married (2) **HELEN HARRESON**.

Notes for David Ross Lindsay:
Bishop of Ross. Called Father of the Church. A man of great ablity and deep learning. Having traveled in France and Switzerland, he imbibed Reformation principles and was one of the twelve Reformation ministers nominated in July 1560, to the "chief places in Scotland," the town of Leith being assigned to him. He was present at the first General Assembly on 20 December 1560, and his name occurs in 50 of the suceeding 73 Assemblies. He visited John Knox on his deathbed in 1572, and at Knox's request, went to the castle of Edinburgh to warn Sir William Kirkcaldy of Grange that unless he gave it up, he "should be

brought down over the walls of it with shame, and hung against the sun" by his political enemies. After his unsuccessful mission, he interceded for Kirkcaldy after his condemnation, attended him on the scafford after intercession failed, and witnessed the literal fufillment of the doom pronounced by Knox. David Lindsay filled a conspicious place in affairs of Church and State, he was "the minister whom the Court liked best."

He accompanied King James to Denmark as Chaplain, and on 23 November 1589 officiated at his wedding to Anne of Denmark at Upsala. He was the only minister of note who had prayers for the beautiful and unhappy Mary, Queen of Scots, at the time of her execution. At the baptism of Prince Henry at Stirling in 1594, he preached to the Ambassadors in French; he also baptized Princess Margaret and Prince Charles (who was to become King).

The testament dative and inventory of the goods, gear, sums of money and debt pertaining to "umquhile Reverend fathyr in God, David, Bishop of Ross, Indweller in Leith the tyme of his deceas, quha deceist in Leith upon the xiiij day of August, the yeire of God, 1613 yeirs," list his son Sir Jerome Lindsay, one of the Comissioners of Edinburgh, as executor dative of the will, and several debts due the late Bishop were listed. Thia was confirmed by the Commissary of Edinburgh on 17 December 1613. *Register of Edinburgh Testamentsl,* CC8/8/56; Scottish Records Office, CC8/8/17.

David Ross Lindsay and Joneta Ramsay had the

following child:

i. JEROME[18] LINDSAY was born in 1562. He died in 1642. He married MARGARET COLVILLE.

Notes for Jerome Lindsay:
Lord Lyon

25. **DAVID[17] LINDSAY** (Rachel, David[14], Walter[13], David[12], David[11], Alexander[10], Catherine[9] Stewart, Stuart Robert[8] II, Marjory[7] Bruce, The Bruce[6] Robert, Robert[5] De Brus, Isabel[4], David Earl of[3] Huntington, Ada[2] De Warenne, William[1] De Warenne) was born in 1531 in Halftoun, Puttorlie, Scotland. He died on 17 Dec 1613 in Annatland, Angusshire, Scotland.

Notes for David Lindsay:
DD, Bishop of Ross, 1600.

David Lindsay had the following child:

17. i. RACHEL LINDSAY was born in 1563. She died on 02 Dec 1639 in Ross, Scotland. She married JOHN SPOTTISWOODE. He was born in 1565. He died on 17 Nov 1639 in London, England.

26. **PATRICK[17] LINDSAY** (John[16], Walter Thomas[15], David[14], Walter[13], David[12], David[11], Alexander[10], Catherine[9] Stewart, Stuart Robert[8] II, Marjory[7] Bruce, The Bruce[6] Robert, Robert[5] De Brus, Isabel[4], David Earl of[3] Huntington, Ada[2] De Warenne, William[1] De Warenne) was born in 1526. He married **ISABELLA PITCAIRN**.

Generation 17 (cont.)

Notes for Patrick Lindsay:
Of Kirkforthar 4th Lord of the Byres. Lindsay was said to have advised the nobles of Scotland to fight at Flodden on 9 September 1513 but sent James IV home. In Pittscottie's story, Lindsay compared the forthcoming encounter to a wager of a gold rose-noble against a bent halfpenny.

He was a reputed advisor of James IV of Scotland, and appointed in December, 1513, counsellor to Margaret Tudor. The arrangement did not last as Margaret married the Earl of Angus and John Stewart, Duke of Albany became regent. In May 1524 Regent Albany appointed Patrick and his son and grandson joint Sheriffs of Fife. Alexander Crawford Lindsay, "Lives of the Lindsays", or "A memoir of the houses of Crawford and Balcarres", vol. 1 (1849), pp. 183-85, 188-9. Macdougall, Norman,"James III", John Donald (1982), p. 283, footnote 19.

Patrick Lindsay and Isabella Pitcairn had the following children:

27.	i.	JAMES[18] LINDSAY was born in 1584 in Melrose Melrose, Roxburgh, Scotland. He died on 11 Oct 1623 in Scotland. He married KATHEREIN GEMMILL.
	ii.	JEAN LINDSAY.
28.	iii.	JOHN LINDSAY.

Generation 18

27\. **JAMES[18] LINDSAY** (Patrick[17], John[16], Walter Thomas[15], David[14], Walter[13], David[12], David[11], Alexander[10],

Generation 18 (cont.)

Catherine^{9} Stewart, Stuart Robert^{8} II, Marjory^{7} Bruce, The Bruce^{6} Robert, Robert^{5} De Brus, Isabel^{4}, David Earl of^{3} Huntington, Ada^{2} De Warenne, William^{1} De Warenne) was born in 1584 in Melrose Melrose, Roxburgh, Scotland. He died on 11 Oct 1623 in Scotland. He married **KATHEREIN GEMMILL**.

James Lindsay and Katherein Gemmill had the following child:

29. i. ALEXANDER^{19} LINDSAY was born in 1610 in Glasgow, Lanarkshire, Scotland. He died about 1718 in Annatland, Angushire Co., Scotland. He married ISOBELL WATSON. She was born in 1613.

28. **JOHN^{18} LINDSAY** (Patrick^{17}, John^{16}, Walter Thomas^{15}, David^{14}, Walter^{13}, David^{12}, David^{11}, Alexander^{10}, Catherine^{9} Stewart, Stuart Robert^{8} II, Marjory^{7} Bruce, The Bruce^{6} Robert, Robert^{5} De Brus, Isabel^{4}, David Earl of^{3} Huntington, Ada^{2} De Warenne, William^{1} De Warenne, Patrick^{17}, John^{16}, Walter^{15}, David^{14}, Walter^{13}, David^{12}, David^{11}, Alexander^{10}, David).

Notes for John Lindsay:
Sir John, Master of Lindsay.

John Lindsay had the following child:

i. JOHN^{19} LINDSAY.

Generation 19

29. **ALEXANDER^{19} LINDSAY** (James^{18}, Patrick^{17}, John^{16}, Walter Thomas^{15}, David^{14}, Walter^{13}, David^{12}, David^{11}, Alexander^{10}, Catherine^{9} Stewart, Stuart Robert^{8} II, Marjory^{7} Bruce, The Bruce^{6} Robert, Robert^{5} De Brus,

Isabel[4], David Earl of[3] Huntington, Ada[2] De Warenne, William[1] De Warenne) was born in 1610 in Glasgow, Lanarkshire, Scotland. He died about 1718 in Annatland, Angushire Co., Scotland. He married **ISOBELL WATSON**. She was born in 1613.

Notes for Alexander Lindsay:
Scotland, Selected Births and Baptisms, 1564-1950; Scotland, Select Marriages, 1561-1910; U.S. and Canada, Passenger and Immigration Lists, 1500s-1900s.

Alexander Lindsay and Isobell Watson had the following child:

30. i. ALEXANDER II[20] LINDSAY was born on 08 Nov 1637 in Lanarkshire, Scotland. He died in 1664 in United States. He married Agnes Thomson Muir, daughter of William Muir and Katherine Henderson Murdoch, in 1663 in Virginia, United States. She was born in Ochiltree, Ayrshire, Scotland. She died in 1684 in Ayrshire, Scotland.

Generation 20

30. **ALEXANDER II[20] LINDSAY** (Alexander[19], James[18], Patrick[17], John[16], Walter Thomas[15], David[14], Walter[13], David[12], David[11], Alexander[10], Catherine[9] Stewart, Stuart Robert[8] II, Marjory[7] Bruce, The Bruce[6] Robert, Robert[5] De Brus, Isabel[4], David Earl of[3] Huntington, Ada[2] De Warenne, William[1] De Warenne) was born on 08 Nov 1637 in Lanarkshire, Scotland. He died in 1664 in United States. He married Agnes Thomson Muir, daughter of William Muir and Katherine

Henderson Murdoch, in 1663 in Virginia, United States. She was born in Ochiltree, Ayrshire, Scotland. She died in 1684 in Ayrshire, Scotland.

Notes for Alexander II Lindsay:
Arrived in Virginia in 1655, age 18. Belfast, Northern Ireland, The Belfast Newsletter Publication January 3, 1905 (Death January 2, 1905) (Birth, Marriage and Death Notices) 1738-1925.

Notes for Agnes Thomson Muir:
Ayrshire & Stirling: The commissariot record of Glasgow Register of testaments, 1547-1800.

Alexander II Lindsay and Agnes Thomson Muir had the following children:

31. i. ALEXANDER III[21] LINDSAY was born on 22 May 1664 in Glasgow, Lanarkshire, Scotland. He died after 1705 in United States. He married (1) JANET RALSTON on 12 Dec 1687 in Glasgow, Lanarkshire, Scotland. She was born in 1663. He married (2) ELIZABETH FARAH on 14 Aug 1690 in Holy Trinity Minories, London, England.

ii. JOHN LINDSAY.

iii. JAMES LINDSAY.

iv. MARTHA LINDSAY.

v. AGNES LINDSAY.

vi. ISOBEL LINDSAY.

Generation 21

Generation 21 (cont.)

31. **ALEXANDER III[21] LINDSAY** (Alexander II[20], Alexander[19], James[18], Patrick[17], John[16], Walter Thomas[15], David[14], Walter[13], David[12], David[11], Alexander[10], Catherine[9] Stewart, Stuart Robert[8] II, Marjory[7] Bruce, The Bruce[6] Robert, Robert[5] De Brus, Isabel[4], David Earl of[3] Huntington, Ada[2] De Warenne, William[1] De Warenne) was born on 22 May 1664 in Glasgow, Lanarkshire, Scotland. He died after 1705 in United States. He married (1) **JANET RALSTON** on 12 Dec 1687 in Glasgow, Lanarkshire, Scotland. She was born in 1663. He married (2) **ELIZABETH FARAH** on 14 Aug 1690 in Holy Trinity Minories, London, England.

Alexander III Lindsay and Janet Ralston had the following children:

i. JOHN[22] LINDSAY was born in 1685.

32. ii. WILLIAM ALEXANDER MALCOLM LINDSAY was born on 16 Jan 1685 in Glasgow, Lanarkshire, Scotland. He died in 1735 in Pennyslvania. He married Janet McCallum, daughter of Neil McCallum and Janet Maxwell, on 24 Nov 1713 in Govan, Lanarkshire, Scotland. She was born on 11 May 1684. She died in 1759.

iii. ALEXANDER (IV) LINDSAY was born in 1688.

Alexander III Lindsay and Elizabeth Farah had the following children:

iv. GEORGE LINDSAY was born in 1691.

v. MARGARET LINDSAY was born in 1693.

Generation 21 (cont.)

vi. THOMAS LINDSAY was born in 1696.

vii. MARY LINDSAY was born in 1698.

viii. JANET LINDSAY was born in 1705.

ix. WILLIAM LINDSAY.

x. ROBERT LINDSAY.

Generation 22

32. **WILLIAM ALEXANDER MALCOLM[22] LINDSAY** (Alexander III[21], Alexander II[20], Alexander[19], James[18], Patrick[17], John[16], Walter Thomas[15], David[14], Walter[13], David[12], David[11], Alexander[10], Catherine[9] Stewart, Stuart Robert[8] II, Marjory[7] Bruce, The Bruce[6] Robert, Robert[5] De Brus, Isabel[4], David Earl of[3] Huntington, Ada[2] De Warenne, William[1] De Warenne) was born on 16 Jan 1685 in Glasgow, Lanarkshire, Scotland. He died in 1735 in Pennyslvania. He married Janet McCallum, daughter of Neil McCallum and Janet Maxwell, on 24 Nov 1713 in Govan, Lanarkshire, Scotland. She was born on 11 May 1684. She died in 1759.

Notes for William Alexander Malcolm Lindsay:
Arrivals: 1719 New Hampshire; 1735 Philadelphia, Pennsylvania.

William Alexander Malcolm Lindsay and Janet McCallum had the following children:

i. ANDREW[23] LINDSAY was born in 1716.

ii. ROBERT LINDSAY was born in 1718.

33. iii. JAMES LINDSAY was born on 26 Nov 1721 in Glasgow, Borony, Scotland.

Generation 22 (cont.)

He died on 02 Nov 1820 in Ohio, Allegheny, Pennsylvania. He married Margaret Hamilton, daughter of James Hamilton and Jean Arneill, on 22 Oct 1747 in East Kilbride, Lanarkshire, Scotland. She was born in 1727 in Govan, Lanarkshire, Scotland (Christening: 06 Oct 1728). She died in 1788.

Generation 23

33. **JAMES[23] LINDSAY** (William Alexander Malcolm[22], Alexander III[21], Alexander II[20], Alexander[19], James[18], Patrick[17], John[16], Walter Thomas[15], David[14], Walter[13], David[12], David[11], Alexander[10], Catherine[9] Stewart, Stuart Robert[8] II, Marjory[7] Bruce, The Bruce[6] Robert, Robert[5] De Brus, Isabel[4], David Earl of[3] Huntington, Ada[2] De Warenne, William[1] De Warenne) was born on 26 Nov 1721 in Glasgow, Borony, Scotland. He died on 02 Nov 1820 in Ohio, Allegheny, Pennsylvania. He married Margaret Hamilton, daughter of James Hamilton and Jean Arneill, on 22 Oct 1747 in East Kilbride, Lanarkshire, Scotland. She was born in 1727 in Govan, Lanarkshire, Scotland (Christening: 06 Oct 1728). She died in 1788.

Notes for James Lindsay:
Baptism: December 17, 1721, St. Sepulchre, London, England.
Arrival age 4 Pennsylvania 1725.
He entered the Revolutionary War army, and died in the service.

Residences: 1770 Nether Providence, Chester

County, Pennsylvania; 1798-1820 Union, Fayette, Pennsylvania.

James Lindsay and Margaret Hamilton had the following children:

34. i. WILLIAM S.[24] LINDSEY was born on 28 Dec 1771 in Glasgow, Lanarkshire, Scotland. He died on 19 Feb 1837 in Pike, Knox County, Ohio. He married Catherine Leidy Reed-Hoffman, daughter of Jacob Bergy Reed and Magdalena Leidy, in 1792 in New Britain Township,Bucks County, Pennsylvania.. She was born in 1770 in Philadelphia, Montgomery, Pennsylvania. She died in 1844 in Perrysville, Ashland, Ohio.

ii. JAMES LINDSEY was born in 1772 in Ohio, Allegheny, Pennsylvania.

iii. PASTELL LINDSEY was born in 1772 in Ohio, Allegheny, Pennsylvania.

Generation 24

34. **WILLIAM S.[24] LINDSEY** (James[23] Lindsay, William Alexander Malcolm[22] Lindsay, Alexander III[21] Lindsay, Alexander II[20] Lindsay, Alexander[19] Lindsay, James[18] Lindsay, Patrick[17] Lindsay, John[16] Lindsay, Walter Thomas[15] Lindsay, David[14] Lindsay, Walter[13] Lindsay, David[12] Lindsay, David[11] Lindsay, Alexander[10] Lindsay, Catherine[9] Stewart, Stuart Robert[8] II, Marjory[7] Bruce, The Bruce[6] Robert, Robert[5] De Brus, Isabel[4], David Earl of[3] Huntington, Ada[2] De Warenne, William[1] De Warenne) was born on 28 Dec 1771 in

Glasgow, Lanarkshire, Scotland. He died on 19 Feb 1837 in Pike, Knox County, Ohio. He married Catherine Leidy Reed-Hoffman, daughter of Jacob Bergy Reed and Magdalena Leidy, in 1792 in New Britain Township,Bucks County, Pennsylvania.. She was born in 1770 in Philadelphia, Montgomery, Pennsylvania. She died in 1844 in Perrysville, Ashland, Ohio.

Notes for William S. Lindsey:
Baptism: January 1, 1760, Glasgow, Lanarkshire, Scotland; Naturalization Declaration July 20, 1827, Pennsylvania; Residence 1820-1837, Pike, Knox County, Ohio.

William S. Lindsey and Catherine Leidy Reed-Hoffman had the following children:

- i. ELIZABETH[25] LINDSEY-KARIGER was born in 1789. She died in 1871.
- ii. JACOB LINDSEY was born in 1795. He died in 1839.
- iii. CATHARINE 'CATY' LINDSEY was born in 1796. She died in 1878.
- iv. MARY E. LINDSEY-BUTLER was born in 1799. She died in 1870.
- v. NANCY LINDSEY-VIRSE was born in 1800. She died in 1883.
- vi. SARAH ELIZABETH LINDSEY was born in 1803. She died in 1893.
- vii. EVE LINDSEY-MCGINLEY was born in 1806. She died in 1893.
- viii. JOHN LINDSEY was born in 1810.

Generation 24 (cont.)

ix. BARBARA LINDSEY was born in 1811 in Stark County, Ohio. She died in 1838.

x. WILLIAM LINDSEY was born in Jul 1813 in Stark County, Ohio. He died (Twin to Susan).

35. xi. SUSAN LINDSEY-PHIFER was born on 13 Jul 1813 in Stark County, Ohio (Twin to William Lindsey). Susan died on 18 Nov 1876 in Loudon, Fayette, Illinois (Burial Mount Moriah Cemetery). Susan married Cornelius B. Phifer on 17 Dec 1828 in Knox County, Ohio. He was born in 1804. He died in 1884.

Generation 25

35. **SUSAN[25] LINDSEY-PHIFER** (William S.[24] Lindsey, James[23] Lindsay, William Alexander Malcolm[22] Lindsay, Alexander III[21] Lindsay, Alexander II[20] Lindsay, Alexander[19] Lindsay, James[18] Lindsay, Patrick[17] Lindsay, John[16] Lindsay, Walter Thomas[15] Lindsay, David[14] Lindsay, Walter[13] Lindsay, David[12] Lindsay, David[11] Lindsay, Alexander[10] Lindsay, Catherine[9] Stewart, Stuart Robert[8] II, Marjory[7] Bruce, The Bruce[6] Robert, Robert[5] De Brus, Isabel[4], David Earl of[3] Huntington, Ada[2] De Warenne, William[1] De Warenne) was born on 13 Jul 1813 in Stark County, Ohio (Twin to William Lindsey). Susan died on 18 Nov 1876 in Loudon, Fayette, Illinois (Burial Mount Moriah Cemetery). Susan married Cornelius B. Phifer on 17 Dec 1828 in Knox County, Ohio. He was born in 1804. He died in 1884.

Cornelius B. Phifer and Susan Lindsey-Phifer had the

following children:

36. i. GEORGE WASHINGTON[26] PHIFER was born in 1829. He died in 1909. He married Ellen Townsend on 28 Nov 1852 in Effingham, Illinois, USA. She was born in 1828 in Effingham, Illinois. She died on 26 Nov 1910 in Bates County, Missouri.

ii. WILLIAM C. PHIFER was born in 1831. He died in 1912.

iii. LUCINDA PHIFER-MOORE was born in 1834. She died in 1915.

iv. EMELINE PHIFER-STAHL was born in 1836. She died in 1915.

v. RACHEL PHIFER-GRANT was born in 1838. She died in 1894.

vi. CHRISTINA ANN PHIFER-HOAR-HOSENEY was born in 1840. She died in 1874.

vii. MARY ELIZABETH PHIFER was born in 1842. She died in 1842.

viii. MARY "CATHERINE" PHIFER-TISH-SPROAT was born in 1848. She died in 1901.

ix. JAMES A. PHIFER was born in 1852. He died in 1914.

x. REBECCA ELLEN PHIFER-BYARD was born in 1852 (Twin to James A. Phifer). She died in 1927.

Generation 26

Generation 26 (cont.)

36. **GEORGE WASHINGTON[26] PHIFER** (Susan[25] Lindsey-Phifer, William S.[24] Lindsey, James[23] Lindsay, William Alexander Malcolm[22] Lindsay, Alexander III[21] Lindsay, Alexander II[20] Lindsay, Alexander[19] Lindsay, James[18] Lindsay, Patrick[17] Lindsay, John[16] Lindsay, Walter Thomas[15] Lindsay, David[14] Lindsay, Walter[13] Lindsay, David[12] Lindsay, David[11] Lindsay, Alexander[10] Lindsay, Catherine[9] Stewart, Stuart Robert[8] II, Marjory[7] Bruce, The Bruce[6] Robert, Robert[5] De Brus, Isabel[4], David Earl of[3] Huntington, Ada[2] De Warenne, William[1] De Warenne) was born in 1829. He died in 1909. He married Ellen Townsend on 28 Nov 1852 in Effingham, Illinois, USA. She was born in 1828 in Effingham, Illinois. She died on 26 Nov 1910 in Bates County, Missouri.

George Washington Phifer and Ellen Townsend had the following children:

37. i. CHRISTINA[27] PHIFER-EWING was born in 1853 in Effingham, Effingham, Illinois, USA. She died in 1928. She married HENRY HARVEY EWING. He was born on 31 Mar 1848 in Wood, Virginia. He died on 10 Mar 1942 in Deer Creek, Bates, Missouri, USA.

ii. WILLIAM A. OR URIAH PHIFER was born in 1858. He died in 1945.

iii. FLORA E. PHIFER-STUBBLEFIELD was born in 1861. She died in 1943 in Bates County, Missouri.

iv. HANNAH PHIFER was born in 1863. She died in 1888 in Bates County, Missouri.

Generation 26 (cont.)

v. FANNY PHIFER was born in 1864.

vi. LEWIS PHIFER was born in 1865. He died in 1865.

vii. MARY ANGELINE PHIFER-HOYT was born in 1868. She died in 1949 in Bates County, Missouri.

viii. GEORGE W. PHIFER JR. was born in 1870. He died in 1965.

ix. LAURA LILLIAN PHIFER-EWING was born in 1872 in Bates County, Missouri. She died in 1966 in California.

Generation 27

37. **CHRISTINA**[27] **PHIFER-EWING** (George Washington[26] Phifer, Susan[25] Lindsey-Phifer, William S.[24] Lindsey, James[23] Lindsay, William Alexander Malcolm[22] Lindsay, Alexander III[21] Lindsay, Alexander II[20] Lindsay, Alexander[19] Lindsay, James[18] Lindsay, Patrick[17] Lindsay, John[16] Lindsay, Walter Thomas[15] Lindsay, David[14] Lindsay, Walter[13] Lindsay, David[12] Lindsay, David[11] Lindsay, Alexander[10] Lindsay, Catherine[9] Stewart, Stuart Robert[8] II, Marjory[7] Bruce, The Bruce[6] Robert, Robert[5] De Brus, Isabel[4], David Earl of[3] Huntington, Ada[2] De Warenne, William[1] De Warenne) was born in 1853 in Effingham, Effingham, Illinois, USA. She died in 1928. She married **HENRY HARVEY EWING**. He was born on 31 Mar 1848 in Wood, Virginia. He died on 10 Mar 1942 in Deer Creek, Bates, Missouri, USA.

Henry Harvey Ewing and Christina Phifer-Ewing had the following children:

Generation 27 (cont.)

38. i. LAURA ELLA[28] EWING was born on 14 Sep 1877 in Effingham, Effingham, Illinois, USA. She died on 29 Aug 1953 in Butler, Bates County, Missouri. She married (1) LEWIS ALVIN DURBIN on 11 Dec 1898 in Effingham, Effingham, Illinois, USA. He was born in 1877 in Effingham, Effingham, Illinois, USA. He died on 18 May 1938 in Adrian, Bates County, Missouri. She married an unknown spouse on 11 Dec 1898 in Altamont, Illinois.

ii. LILIAN FLORENCE EWING was born on 24 Dec 1882 in Moccasin, Effingham. She died in 1965 in Bates County, Missouri.

iii. MARY VIVIAN EWING was born on 26 Feb 1889 in Effingham, Illinois. She died in 1980 in California.

Generation 28

38. **LAURA ELLA[28] EWING** (Christina[27] Phifer-Ewing, George Washington[26] Phifer, Susan[25] Lindsey-Phifer, William S.[24] Lindsey, James[23] Lindsay, William Alexander Malcolm[22] Lindsay, Alexander III[21] Lindsay, Alexander II[20] Lindsay, Alexander[19] Lindsay, James[18] Lindsay, Patrick[17] Lindsay, John[16] Lindsay, Walter Thomas[15] Lindsay, David[14] Lindsay, Walter[13] Lindsay, David[12] Lindsay, David[11] Lindsay, Alexander[10] Lindsay, Catherine[9] Stewart, Stuart Robert[8] II, Marjory[7] Bruce, The Bruce[6] Robert, Robert[5] De Brus, Isabel[4], David Earl of[3] Huntington, Ada[2] De Warenne, William[1] De Warenne) was born on 14 Sep 1877 in

Effingham, Effingham, Illinois, USA. She died on 29 Aug 1953 in Butler, Bates County, Missouri. She married (1) **Lewis Alvin Durbin** on 11 Dec 1898 in Effingham, Effingham, Illinois, USA. He was born in 1877 in Effingham, Effingham, Illinois, USA. He died on 18 May 1938 in Adrian, Bates County, Missouri. She married an unknown spouse on 11 Dec 1898 in Altamont, Illinois.

Laura Ella Ewing had the following child:

39. i. Nellie[29] Barkley was born on 06 Aug 1900 in Cass County, Archie, Missouri. She died on 27 Oct 1948 in Shawnee, Bates County, Missouri.

Lewis Alvin Durbin and Laura Ella Ewing had the following children:

i. Leslie Alvin[29] Durbin was born on 11 Oct 1908 in Bates County, Missouri. He died on 27 Sep 1952 in Adrian, Bates County, Missouri.

ii. Jesse William Durbin was born in 1911 in Bates County, Missouri.

iii. Ufa Henry Durbin.

Generation 29

39. **Nellie[29] Barkley** (Laura Ella[28] Ewing, Christina[27] Phifer-Ewing, George Washington[26] Phifer, Susan[25] Lindsey-Phifer, William S.[24] Lindsey, James[23] Lindsay, William Alexander Malcolm[22] Lindsay, Alexander III[21] Lindsay, Alexander II[20] Lindsay, Alexander[19] Lindsay, James[18] Lindsay, Patrick[17] Lindsay, John[16] Lindsay, Walter Thomas[15] Lindsay,

Generation 29 (cont.)

David[14] Lindsay, Walter[13] Lindsay, David[12] Lindsay, David[11] Lindsay, Alexander[10] Lindsay, Catherine[9] Stewart, Stuart Robert[8] II, Marjory[7] Bruce, The Bruce[6] Robert, Robert[5] De Brus, Isabel[4], David Earl of[3] Huntington, Ada[2] De Warenne, William[1] De Warenne) was born on 06 Aug 1900 in Cass County, Archie, Missouri. She died on 27 Oct 1948 in Shawnee, Bates County, Missouri.

Nellie Barkley had the following children:

i. MARVIN DARRELL DURBIN was born in 1924 in Bates County, Missouri. He died in 1992 in Seattle, Washinton.

ii. JACK CALVIN DURBIN was born on 23 Sep 1925 in Bates County, Missouri. He died in 2012 in Wichita, Sedgwick, Kansas, USA.

iii. LEONARD LEROY DURBIN was born on 20 Aug 1927 in Archie, Cass, Missouri. He died in 1995 in Butler, Bates County, Missouri.

iv. BETTY JEWELL DURBIN was born on 02 Feb 1931 in Shawnee, Bates County, Missouri. She married WINFRED LEE CARSON SR..

v. DORIS MAY DURBIN was born on 11 Aug 1932 in Adrian, Missouri (Shawnee Twp, Bates County, Missouri). She died in Manvel, Brazoria, Texas (Ashes scattered, Happy, Texas). She married Ovid Maurice Wooley, son of Ovid Garlington Wooley and Mildred

Maurine Walker, on 17 Feb 1952 in Wichita, Sedgwick, Kansas, USA (At home of brother Jack & Maedean.). He was born on 03 Jul 1933 in Happy, Texas. He died on 05 Nov 2004 in Caynon, Happy, Texas.

Notes for Doris May Durbin:
Cremated, ashes scattered on old home place, Happy, Texas.

vi. PEGGY JOYCE DURBIN was born on 02 Jul 1936 in Shawnee, Bates County, Missouri. She married IRVIN LEE BEERY.

vii. CAROL JEAN DURBIN was born on 01 Jul 1940 in Shawnee, Bates County, Missouri. She married Arthur Bidner on 03 Mar 1962 in Kansas City, Missouri. He was born on 17 Feb 1932 in Brooklyn, New York.

Descendants of Mathuedol Count of Poher de Bretagne

Generation 1

1. **Mathuedol Count Of Poher[1] De Bretagne** was born in 875 AD in Dinah, Ille-et-Vilaine, Bretagne, France. He died in 952 AD in Bretagne, Normandy, France. He married **Oreguen De Vannes**. She was born in 882 AD. She died in 947 AD.

   Mathuedol Count of Poher de Bretagne and Oreguen de Vannes had the following child:

   2. i. Alain Ii[2] Strongbeard. He married Roscille De Bretagne D'Anjou.

Generation 2

2. **Alain Ii[2] Strongbeard** (Mathuedol Count of Poher[1] de Bretagne). He married **Roscille De Bretagne D'Anjou**.

   Alain II Strongbeard and Roscille De Bretagne D'Anjou had the following child:

   3. i. Hamon[3] De Dinah. He married Rantlina Bretagne.

Generation 3

3. **Hamon[3] De Dinah** (Alain II[2] Strongbeard, Mathuedol Count of Poher[1] de Bretagne). He married **Rantlina Bretagne**.

   Hamon de Dinah and Rantlina Bretagne had the following child:

   4. i. Dapifer De Dol[4] Flaald. He married Muldivane De Atholl.

Generation 4

4. **Dapifer De Dol[4] Flaald** (Hamon[3] de Dinah, Alain II[2] Strongbeard, Mathuedol Count of Poher[1] de Bretagne). He married **Muldivane De Atholl**.

Generation 4 (cont.)

Dapifer de Dol Flaald and Muldivane de Atholl had the following child:

5. i. ALAN FITZ[5] FLAAID was born in 1020 in Dol De Bretagne, Ile-et-Viaine, Bretagne, France. He died in 1080 in Jerusalem, Yerushalayim, Israel. He married Nesta Verch Gruffydd in 1037. She was born in 1024. She died in 1152.

Generation 5

5. **ALAN FITZ[5] FLAAID** (Dapifer de Dol[4] Flaald, Hamon[3] de Dinah, Alain II[2] Strongbeard, Mathuedol Count of Poher[1] de Bretagne) was born in 1020 in Dol De Bretagne, Ile-et-Viaine, Bretagne, France. He died in 1080 in Jerusalem, Yerushalayim, Israel. He married Nesta Verch Gruffydd in 1037. She was born in 1024. She died in 1152.

Alan Fitz Flaaid and Nesta Verch Gruffydd had the following children:

6. i. GUENTA VERCH[6] GRIFFITH was born in 1050. She died in 1084. She married FITZ ALAN FLAAID. He was born in 1046. He died in 1103.

7. ii. ALAN FITZ FLAAD was born in 1078 in Dol, Ill et Vilaine, Bretagne, France. He died in 1114 in Oswestry, Shropshire, England. He married Aveline de Hesdin, daughter of Fitz Alan Flaaid and Guenta Verch Griffith, in 1105 in Dol De Bretagne, Ile-et-Viaine, Bretagne, France. She was born in 1081. She died in 1126 in Shropshire, England.

Generation 6

6. **GUENTA VERCH[6] GRIFFITH** (Alan Fitz[5] Flaaid, Dapifer de Dol[4] Flaald, Hamon[3] de Dinah, Alain II[2] Strongbeard, Mathuedol

Count of Poher[1] de Bretagne) was born in 1050. She died in 1084. She married **Fitz Alan Flaaid**. He was born in 1046. He died in 1103.

Fitz Alan Flaaid and Guenta Verch Griffith had the following children:

8. i. Aveline[7] De Hesdin was born in 1081. She died in 1126 in Shropshire, England. She married Alan Fitz Flaad, son of Alan Fitz Flaaid and Nesta Verch Gruffydd, in 1105 in Dol De Bretagne, Ile-et-Viaine, Bretagne, France. He was born in 1078 in Dol, Ill et Vilaine, Bretagne, France. He died in 1114 in Oswestry, Shropshire, England.

ii. William Fitz Alan Stewart Flaad was born in 1105. He died in 1160.

iii. Walter Fitz Alan Flaad was born in 1109. He died in 1174.

7. **Alan Fitz[6] Flaad** (Alan Fitz[5] Flaaid, Dapifer de Dol[4] Flaald, Hamon[3] de Dinah, Alain II[2] Strongbeard, Mathuedol Count of Poher[1] de Bretagne) was born in 1078 in Dol, Ill et Vilaine, Bretagne, France. He died in 1114 in Oswestry, Shropshire, England. He married Aveline de Hesdin, daughter of Fitz Alan Flaaid and Guenta Verch Griffith, in 1105 in Dol De Bretagne, Ile-et-Viaine, Bretagne, France. She was born in 1081. She died in 1126 in Shropshire, England.

Notes for Alan Fitz Flaad:
A Breton knight, probably recruited as a mercenary by Henry I of England in his conflict with his brothers.

Alan's rapid descent to wealth and power was a symptom of troubled times. The abortive revolt of Robert de Belleme in 1102 had torn apart the Anglo-Norman system of governing the Welsh Marches. With other Breton friends, Alan had been given forfeited lands in Norfolk and Shropshire, including some which had previously belonged to Robert de Belleme himself (Ritchie, 1954, pp. 280-281).

Not until the first decade of the 19th century did George Chalmers defintely prove that Walter Fitz Alan, an acknowledged link in the Stewart ancestry, came from Shropshire and was actually the son of Alan Fitz Flaad. This finally established Alan Fitz Flaad's existence and importance and confirmed the kinship between the Stewarts and the FitzAlan Earls of Arundel (Chambers, Volume 2, pp. 572-3).

Notes for Aveline de Hesdin:
Daughter of Ernulf de Hesdin, a tenant-in-chief in ten counties at the time of Domesday (Round, 1899), who was killed on crusade at Antioch (Round, 1901; Richie 1954, p. 98n). The Burke's *Royal Families* of 1848 was one of the sources that asserted Alan's wife was the "daughter and heir of Warine, Sheriff of Shropshire, *temp*, William the Conqueror." (Burke, John and John Bernard, Volume 2, p. xl).

Alan Fitz Flaad and Aveline de Hesdin had the following child:

9. i. ALAN FITZ WALTER[7] STEWART was born in 1126 in East Ayrshire, Scotland. He died in 1204 in Dundonald, Kyle, Ayshire, Scotland. He married Margaret de Galloway, daughter of Walter Fitz Alan Stewart and Eschyna De Molle, in 1165 in Carrick, Ayeshire, Scotland. She was born in 1132 in England. She died on 22 Sep 1182 in East Ayrshire, Scotland.

Generation 7

Generation 7 (cont.)

8. **Aveline**[7] **De Hesdin** (Guenta Verch[6] Griffith, Alan Fitz[5] Flaaid, Dapifer de Dol[4] Flaald, Hamon[3] de Dinah, Alain II[2] Strongbeard, Mathuedol Count of Poher[1] de Bretagne) was born in 1081. She died in 1126 in Shropshire, England. She married Alan Fitz Flaad, son of Alan Fitz Flaaid and Nesta Verch Gruffydd, in 1105 in Dol De Bretagne, Ile-et-Viaine, Bretagne, France. He was born in 1078 in Dol, Ill et Vilaine, Bretagne, France. He died in 1114 in Oswestry, Shropshire, England.

   Notes for Aveline de Hesdin:
   Daughter of Ernulf de Hesdin, a tenant-in-chief in ten counties at the time of Domesday (Round, 1899), who was killed on crusade at Antioch (Round, 1901; Richie 1954, p. 98n). The Burke's *Royal Families* of 1848 was one of the sources that asserted Alan's wife was the "daughter and heir of Warine, Sheriff of Shropshire, *temp*, William the Conqueror." (Burke, John and John Bernard, Volume 2, p. xl).

   Notes for Alan Fitz Flaad:
   A Breton knight, probably recruited as a mercenary by Henry I of England in his conflict with his brothers.

   Alan's rapid descent to wealth and power was a symptom of troubled times. The abortive revolt of Robert de Belleme in 1102 had torn apart the Anglo-Norman system of governing the Welsh Marches. With other Breton friends, Alan had been given forfeited lands in Norfolk and Shropshire, including some which had previously belonged to Robert de Belleme himself (Ritchie, 1954, pp. 280-281).

   Not until the first decade of the 19th century did George Chalmers defintely prove that Walter Fitz Alan, an acknowledged link in the Stewart ancestry, came from Shropshire and was actually the son of Alan Fitz Flaad. This finally established Alan Fitz Flaad's existence and importance and confirmed the kinship between the Stewarts and the FitzAlan Earls of Arundel (Chambers, Volume 2, pp. 572-3).

Alan Fitz Flaad and Aveline de Hesdin had the following child:

9. i. ALAN FITZ WALTER[7] STEWART was born in 1126 in East Ayrshire, Scotland. He died in 1204 in Dundonald, Kyle, Ayshire, Scotland. He married Margaret de Galloway, daughter of Walter Fitz Alan Stewart and Eschyna De Molle, in 1165 in Carrick, Ayeshire, Scotland. She was born in 1132 in England. She died on 22 Sep 1182 in East Ayrshire, Scotland.

9. **ALAN FITZ WALTER[7] STEWART** (Alan Fitz[6] Flaad, Alan Fitz[5] Flaaid, Dapifer de Dol[4] Flaald, Hamon[3] de Dinah, Alain II[2] Strongbeard, Mathuedol Count of Poher[1] de Bretagne) was born in 1126 in East Ayrshire, Scotland. He died in 1204 in Dundonald, Kyle, Ayshire, Scotland. He married Margaret de Galloway, daughter of Walter Fitz Alan Stewart and Eschyna De Molle, in 1165 in Carrick, Ayeshire, Scotland. She was born in 1132 in England. She died on 22 Sep 1182 in East Ayrshire, Scotland.

Alan Fitz Walter Stewart and Margaret de Galloway had the following children:

i. AVELINA FITZ WALTER[8] STEWART was born in 1179. She died in 1204.

10. ii. WALTER FITZ ALAN STEWART was born in 1180. He died in 1246. He married (1) UNKNOWN.

iii. BEATRICE GILCHREST was born in 1184. She died in 1270. She married WALTER FITZ ALAN STEWART.

iv. EUPHEMIA STEWART was born in 1206 in Dunbar, Haddington, Lincolnshire,

Scotland. She died in 1267.

v. MARGARET ISABEL FITZ ALAN STEWART was born in 1206 in Dundonald, Kyle, Ayshire, Scotland. She died in 1292.

vi. JOHN STEWART was born in 1216 in Dundonald, Kyle, Ayshire, Scotland. He died in 1249.

vii. WALTERBALLIOCH STEWART was born in 1218 in Dundonald, Kyle, Ayshire, Scotland. He died in 1296 in Dundonald Castle, Irvine, East Ayrshire, Scotland.

Generation 8

10. **WALTER FITZ ALAN**[8] **STEWART** (Alan Fitz Walter[7], Alan Fitz[6] Flaad, Alan Fitz[5] Flaaid, Dapifer de Dol[4] Flaald, Hamon[3] de Dinah, Alain II[2] Strongbeard, Mathuedol Count of Poher[1] de Bretagne) was born in 1180. He died in 1246. He married (1) **UNKNOWN**.

Notes for Walter Fitz Alan Stewart:
Great, great grandfather of William Wallace.

Walter Fitz Alan Stewart had the following child:

11. i. ALEXANDER[9] STEWART was born in 1197 in Castle Dundonald, Ayshire, Scotland. He died in 1283 in Castle Irvine, Ayshire, Scotland. He married (1) JEAN MACRORY in 1242 in Dundonald, Kyle, Ayshire, Scotland. She was born in 1218 in Scotland. She died in 1250 in Castle Irvine, Ayshire, Scotland.

Walter Fitz Alan Stewart and Unknown had the following child:

12. ii. BEATRIX GILCHREST was born in 1184 in Scotland. She died in 1270 in Forfar,

Angus, , Scotland. She married WALTER "OG" STEWART.

Generation 9

11. **ALEXANDER[9] STEWART** (Walter Fitz Alan[8], Alan Fitz Walter[7], Alan Fitz[6] Flaad, Alan Fitz[5] Flaaid, Dapifer de Dol[4] Flaald, Hamon[3] de Dinah, Alain II[2] Strongbeard, Mathuedol Count of Poher[1] de Bretagne) was born in 1197 in Castle Dundonald, Ayshire, Scotland. He died in 1283 in Castle Irvine, Ayshire, Scotland. He married (1) **JEAN MACRORY** in 1242 in Dundonald, Kyle, Ayshire, Scotland. She was born in 1218 in Scotland. She died in 1250 in Castle Irvine, Ayshire, Scotland.

Alexander Stewart had the following child:

i. WALTER[10] STEWART. He married BETHOC (BEATRIX) CRIST.

Alexander Stewart and Jean Macrory had the following children:

ii. ALEXANDER STUART was born in 1240. He died on 16 Jul 1309 in Y, Somme, Picardie, France.

13. iii. JAMES LAIRD OF GARLIES STUART was born in 1243 in Irvine, East Ayrshire, Scotland. He died on 16 Jul 1309 in Irvine, East Ayrshire, Scotland. He married (1) EGIDIA GILES DE BURGH in 1292 in Kyle, Ayrshire, Scotland. She was born in 1257 in Kyle, Ayrshire, Scotland. She died in 1327.

iv. ELIZABETH STUART was born in 1245 in Irvine, East Ayrshire, Scotland. She died in 1288.

v. JOHN LORD BONKYL STUART was born in Apr 1246 in Dundonald, Kyle, Ayshire, Scotland. He died on 22 Jul 1289 in

Stirlingshire, Scotland (The Battle of Falkirk under William Wallace).

vi. HAWISE STUART was born in 1258 in Irvine, Ayrshire, Scotland. She died in 1358 in Irvine, Ayrshire, Scotland.

12. **BEATRIX[9] GILCHREST** (Walter Fitz Alan[8] Stewart, Alan Fitz Walter[7] Stewart, Alan Fitz[6] Flaad, Alan Fitz[5] Flaaid, Dapifer de Dol[4] Flaald, Hamon[3] de Dinah, Alain II[2] Strongbeard, Mathuedol Count of Poher[1] de Bretagne) was born in 1184 in Scotland. She died in 1270 in Forfar, Angus, , Scotland. She married **WALTER "OG" STEWART**.

Notes for Walter "Og" Stewart:
Walter "Og" Stewart

Walter "Og" Stewart and Beatrix Gilchrest had the following child:

i. WALTER[10] STEWART. He married BETHOC (BEATRIX) CRIST.

Generation 10

13. **JAMES LAIRD OF GARLIES[10] STUART** (Alexander[9] Stewart, Walter Fitz Alan[8] Stewart, Alan Fitz Walter[7] Stewart, Alan Fitz[6] Flaad, Alan Fitz[5] Flaaid, Dapifer de Dol[4] Flaald, Hamon[3] de Dinah, Alain II[2] Strongbeard, Mathuedol Count of Poher[1] de Bretagne) was born in 1243 in Irvine, East Ayrshire, Scotland. He died on 16 Jul 1309 in Irvine, East Ayrshire, Scotland. He married (1) **EGIDIA GILES DE BURGH** in 1292 in Kyle, Ayrshire, Scotland. She was born in 1257 in Kyle, Ayrshire, Scotland. She died in 1327.

James Laird of Garlies Stuart had the following child:

14. i. UNKNOWN[11]. She married ANDREW STEWART. He was born in 1290 in Irvine Burgh, Ayrshire, Scotland. He died in 1309.

Generation 11

Generation 11 (cont.)

14. **UNKNOWN**[11] (James Laird of Garlies[10] Stuart, Alexander[9] Stewart, Walter Fitz Alan[8] Stewart, Alan Fitz Walter[7] Stewart, Alan Fitz[6] Flaad, Alan Fitz[5] Flaaid, Dapifer de Dol[4] Flaald, Hamon[3] de Dinah, Alain II[2] Strongbeard, Mathuedol Count of Poher[1] de Bretagne). She married **ANDREW STEWART**. He was born in 1290 in Irvine Burgh, Ayrshire, Scotland. He died in 1309.

Andrew Stewart and Unknown had the following child:

15. i. JAMES[12] STEWART. He married MARY OF GUELDRES.

Generation 12

15. **JAMES[12] STEWART** (Unknown[11], James Laird of Garlies[10] Stuart, Alexander[9], Walter Fitz Alan[8], Alan Fitz Walter[7], Alan Fitz[6] Flaad, Alan Fitz[5] Flaaid, Dapifer de Dol[4] Flaald, Hamon[3] de Dinah, Alain II[2] Strongbeard, Mathuedol Count of Poher[1] de Bretagne, Andrew, James, Alexander Stuart). He married **MARY OF GUELDRES**.

Notes for Mary of Gueldres:
Mary passed away on December 1, 1363, in Roxborough Castle, Roxboroughshire, Scotland, age 30.

James Stewart and Mary of Gueldres had the following child:

i. JAMES III[13] STEWART. He married Margaret Oldenburg in 1469 in Holyrood, Edinburgh Mislothian,Scotland. She was born in 1456 in Denmark. She died in 1486 in Holyrood, Edinburgh Mislothian,Scotland.

Descendants of Walter Alexander Stewart

Generation 1

1. **WALTER ALEXANDER[1] STEWART** was born in 1214 in Scotland Gate, Northumberland, England. He died in 1283. He married **BETHOC (BEATRIX) MAC GILLE CRIST**.

   Notes for Walter Alexander Stewart:
   3rd High Steward of Scotland. Coat of Arms: Or, fess chequy orgent and azure. Alexander is said to have accompanied Louis IX of France on the Seventh Crusade (1248-1254). In 1255 he was one of the councillors of King Alexander III, though under age. Anderson, William, "The Scottish Nation", Edinburgh, 1867, vol. ix, p. 512. He was the principal commander under King Alexander III of Scotland at the Battle of Largys on 2 October 1263, when the Scots defeated the Norwegians under Haakon IV. The Scots invaded and conquered the Isle of Man the following year, which was, with the whole of the Western Isles, then annexed to the Crown of Scotland. Burke, Messrs., John and John Barnard, "The Royal Families of England, Scotland, and Wales,, with their descendants", vol. 2, London, 1851, pp. xli-xlii. Anderson (1867), Ibid.

   Through his eldest son James, Alexander was a great-grandfather of King Robert II, the first Stewart to be King of Scots, and thus ancestors of all subsequent Scottish monarchs and the later and current monarchs of Great Britain.
   Through his second son John, Alexander was a parilineal ancester of Henry Stuart, Lord Darnley, and of the Stuart monarchs of Scotland and England from Darlent's son James VI and I onwards. Simpson, David. "The Genealogical and Chronicle History of

Generation 1 (cont.)

Edinburgh, 1713." Patrilineality, also known as the male line, the spear side or agnatic kinship, is a common kinship system in which an individual's family membership derives from and is recorded through their father's lineage. It generally involves the inheritance of property, rights, names, or titles by persons related through male kin. This is sometimes distinguished from cognate kinship, through the mother's lineage, also called the spindle side or the distaff side.
(Wikipedia)

Walter Alexander Stewart and Bethoc (Beatrix) Mac Gille Crist had the following children:

i. JOHN[2] STEWART was born in 1245 in Bonkill, Berksshire, Scotland. He died on 22 Jul 1298 in Killed in Battle of Falkirk.. He married BOMKILL HEIRESS.

Notes for John Stewart:
Agnatic ancestor of British Kings.
Agnatic seniority is a patrilineal principle of inheritance where the order of succession to the throne prefers the monarch's younger brother over the monarch's own sons. A monarch's children succeed only after the males of the elder generation have all been exhausted. Agnatic seniority essentially excludes females of the dynasty and their descendants from the succession. Contrast agnatic primogeniture, where the king's sons

Generation 1 (cont.)

stand higher in succession than his brothers.

2. ii. JAMES STEWART was born in 1260 in Kilmarnock, East Ayshire, Scotland. He died on 16 Jul 1309 in Irvine, Ayrshire, Scotland (Burial: Paisley Abbey, Renfrewshire, Scotland). He married Egidia Giles de Burgh in 1290 in Kyle, Ayrshire, Scotland. She was born in 1257 in Kyle, Ayrshire, Scotland. She died in 1327.

Generation 2

2. **JAMES[2] STEWART** (Walter Alexander[1]) was born in 1260 in Kilmarnock, East Ayshire, Scotland. He died on 16 Jul 1309 in Irvine, Ayrshire, Scotland (Burial: Paisley Abbey, Renfrewshire, Scotland). He married Egidia Giles de Burgh in 1290 in Kyle, Ayrshire, Scotland. She was born in 1257 in Kyle, Ayrshire, Scotland. She died in 1327.

Notes for James Stewart:
Last name spelled Stewart versus Stuart. 5th High Steward of Scotland was High Steward of Scotland and a guardian of Scotland during the First Interregnum. In 1286 James was chosen as one of the six Guardians of Scotland. He subsequently submitted to King Edward I of England on 9 July 1297, and was one of the auditors for the competitor, Robert Bruce, 5th Lord of Annandale. However, during the Wars of Scottish Independence he joined Sir William Wallace. After Wallace's defeat at the

Generation 2 (cont.)

Battle of Falkirk in 1298, he gave his support to Robert Bruce, later King Robert I of Scotland, grandson of the competitor.

In 1302, with six other ambassdors incuding John Comyn, Earl of Buchan, he was sent to solicit the aid of the French king against Edward, to whom he was once again compelled to swear fealty at Lanercost on 23 October 1306. To render his oath if possible secure, it was taken upon the two crosses of Scotland most esteemed for their sanctity, on the consecrated host, the holy gospels, and certain relics of saints. He also agreed to submit to instant excommunication if he should break his allegiance to Edward. Convinced that his faith was to his country in spite of all, he once again took up the Scottish patriotic cause and died in the service of The Bruce in 1309.

James Stewart and Egidia Giles de Burgh had the following children:

3. i. ANDREW STEWART was born in 1290 in Irvine Burgh, Ayrshire, Scotland. He died in 1309. He married UNKNOWN.

ii. JOHN STEWART was born in 1294 in Angus, Scotland. He died in 1331.

4. iii. WALTER STEWART was born on 11 Jul 1294 in Dundonald, Kyle, Ayshire, Scotland. He died on 09 Apr 1326 in Scotland. He married Marjorie Bruce, daughter of Robert Bruce and Isabel de Clare, in 1315. She was born in Scotland. She died on 02 Mar 1316 in

Generation 2 (cont.)

Scotland.

iv. EGIDIA STEWART.

Generation 3

3. **ANDREW STEWART** (James[2], Walter Alexander[1]) was born in 1290 in Irvine Burgh, Ayrshire, Scotland. He died in 1309. He married **UNKNOWN**.

Andrew Stewart and Unknown had the following child:

5. i. JAMES STEWART. He married MARY OF GUELDRES.

4. **WALTER[3] STEWART** (James[2], Walter Alexander[1]) was born on 11 Jul 1294 in Dundonald, Kyle, Ayshire, Scotland. He died on 09 Apr 1326 in Scotland. He married Marjorie Bruce, daughter of Robert Bruce and Isabel de Clare, in 1315. She was born in Scotland. She died on 02 Mar 1316 in Scotland.

Notes for Walter Stewart:
6th High Steward of Scotland. The Stewart Clan claims its traditional descent from Banquo, Thane of Lochaber, who features in Shapespeare's play, Macbeth. However, the Stewart family who became kings of Scotland historically descended from a family who for at least four generations were seneschals (royal stewards) of Dol near Mont-Saint-Michel in Britany, France. A plaque in Dol today commerates that origin. The stewards of Dol in return reputed to have been descended from Froamidus, Count of Brittany, who lived in the middle of the eighth century.

Walter Stewart, son of James, fought on the side of

Generation 3 (cont.)

Robert the Bruce at the great Scottish victory at Bannockburn in 1314, commanding along with Douglas, the left-wing of the Scots' Army. He was the nominial leader of one of the four Scottish schiktrons, but because of his youth and inexperience, the effective leader was his cousin James Douglas, Lord of Douglas. Walter was dispatched to the English border to receive Robert the Bruce's wife and daughter from their long captivity in England and conducted them back to the Scottish Court. During Robert's campaign in Ireland he and Sir James Douglas managed government affairs and spent much time defending the Scottish borders.

Folling the capture of Berwick-upon-Tweed from the English in 1318, he was given command of the town which, on 24 July 1319 was beseiged by King Edward II of England. Several of the seige engines were destroyed by the Scots' garrison and The Steward suddenly rushed in force from the town to drive off the enemy. In 1322, with Douglas and Thomas Randolph, he attempted to surprise the English King at Byland Abbey, near Malton, Yorkshire. Edward, however, escaped, pursued towards York by The Steward anf 500 horsemen.

The Stewarts first came to Britain after the Norman conquest, when they were invited to England by King Henry I, son of William the Conqueror. King Henry granted them estates in England in Shropshire and Norfolk. *Wikipedia, The Free Encloypedia.*

Generation 3 (cont.)

Notes for Marjorie Bruce:
Princess Royal Scotland.

Walter Stewart and Marjorie Bruce had the following child:

6. i. ROBERT[4] STEWART was born on 02 Mar 1316 in Dundonald, Kyle, Ayshire, Scotland. He died on 19 Apr 1390 in His Castle of Dundonald, Kyle, Ayrshire, Scotland. He married (1) ELIZABETH MURE, daughter of Adam Muir, in 1347 in Scotland. She was born in 1332 in Scotland. She died in 1387. He married (2) EUPHEMIA DE ROSS on 02 May 1355. She died in 1387.

Generation 4

5. **JAMES STEWART** (Andrew, James[2], Walter Alexander[1], Andrew, James, Alexander Stuart). He married **MARY OF GUELDRES**.

Notes for Mary of Gueldres:
Mary passed away on December 1, 1363, in Roxborough Castle, Roxboroughshire, Scotland, age 30.

James Stewart and Mary of Gueldres had the following child:

i. JAMES III STEWART. He married Margaret Oldenburg in 1469 in Holyrood, Edinburgh Mislothian,Scotland. She was born in

Generation 4 (cont.)

1456 in Denmark. She died in 1486 in Holyrood, Edinburgh Mislothian,Scotland.

6. **ROBERT**[4] **STEWART** (Walter[3], James[2], Walter Alexander[1]) was born on 02 Mar 1316 in Dundonald, Kyle, Ayshire, Scotland. He died on 19 Apr 1390 in His Castle of Dundonald, Kyle, Ayrshire, Scotland. He married (1) **ELIZABETH MURE**, daughter of Adam Muir, in 1347 in Scotland. She was born in 1332 in Scotland. She died in 1387. He married (2) **EUPHEMIA DE ROSS** on 02 May 1355. She died in 1387.

   Notes for Robert Stewart:
   Robert II, also remembered as Robert the Steward and the first monarch of the House of Stewart, was the King of Scots who ruled from 1371 to his death. He was the only child of Walter Stewart, 6th High Steward of Scotland and his first wife Marjorie Bruce, daughter of Robert the Bruce and Isabella of Mar. He was delivered by cesarean section, the heavily pregnant Marjorie Bruce had been riding in Galloway, Paisley, Renfrew when her horse was suddenly startled and threw her to the ground at a place called 'The Knock.' She was seriously injured, her fall caused a dislocation of her neck bone. She went into premature labor who failed to survive the ordeal of a caesaren section, dying a few hour later.

   All of Robert's children by his first wife were born out of wedlock. Elizabeth Mure and Robert had finally married in 1347, but because they were within the forbidden degree of consanguinity, a dispensation

Generation 4 (cont.)

had to be acquired from the church which further legitimized their offspring. Controversy existed as to whether any of the couple's many children could legally succeed to the crown. Robert eventually decided that his heir was to be his firstborn son by Elizabeth; John, Earl of Carrick, (later Robert III) who was also the High Steward of Scotland. The Earl of Carrick, now heir to the throne, was a sickly man with a pronounced limp.

In 1318 a parliament at Scone declared the two-year old as his grandfather's successor, but he was displaced as the heir to the Scottish throne on the birth of Robert's only son, David.

The unruly Scottish barons held little respect for their new King who was considered an old and weak man who failed to exercise strong control over them.

In 1371, when his nephew died childless, Robert finally succeeded to the throne of Scotland at the age of 55. He was crowned at Scone, Perthshire, in March 1371. Reported to have been tall and handsome, in character he was the very antithesis of the famous grandfather whose name he bore. Robert was timid, indecisive and weak-willed.

Robert II deputized the government of the unruly Highlands to his third son, Alexander, Earl of Buchanan, known as the Wolf of Badenoch. Alexander ruled with savagery drawing critism from northern earls and bishops and his half-brother David,

Generation 4 (cont.)

Earl of Strathearn. These complaints damaged the king's standing within the Council leading to criticism of his ability to curb Buchanan's activities.

King Robert had more children than any other King of Scotland, in all 15 by his two marriages. Susan Abernethy (2014-03-22). *Two Wifes of Robert II, King of Scotland - Elizabeth Mure and Euphemia Ross*. The Freelance History Writer.

Title: *March 26, 1371, King Robert of Scotland at Scone.*

Robert Stewart and Elizabeth Mure had the following children:

i. JOHN[5] STEWART was born in 1294 in Angus, Scotland. He died in 1331.

ii. JOHN STEWART was born about 1337 in Scotland. He died in 1406 in Scotland.

7. iii. KATHERINE STEWART. She married DAVID LINDSAY.

iv. WALTER STEWART.

v. ROBERT STEWART.

vi. MARGARET STEWART.

vii. ALEXANDER STEWART.

viii. MARJORIE STEWART.

ix. JEAN STEWART.

x. ISABEL STEWART.

Generation 4 (cont.)

xi. KATHERINE STEWART.

xii. ELIZABETH STEWART.

Notes for Euphemia de Ross:
Queen Consort of Scotland.

Robert Stewart and Euphemia de Ross had the following children:

xiii. WALTER STEWART was born in 1338 in Scotland. He died in 1362 in Scotland.

xiv. DAVID STEWART.

xv. MARGARET STEWART.

xvi. ELIZABETH STEWART. She married DAVID LINDSAY.

xvii. EGIDIA STEWART. She married WILLIAM DOUGLAS. He was born in Nitherdale.

Generation 5

7. **KATHERINE[5] STEWART** (John[5], James[2], Walter Alexander[1], Robert[4], Walter[3], James[2], Walter Alexander[1]). She married **DAVID LINDSAY**.

David Lindsay and Katherine Stewart had the following children:

8. i. DAVID[6] LINDSAY was born in 1410 in Crawford, Lanarkshire, Scotland. He died on 17 Jan 1446 in Angusshire, Scotland, Battle of Aberbrothock.. He married MARGORIE OGILVIE. She was born in 1410. She died in 1476.

Generation 5 (cont.)

9. ii. ALEXANDER LINDSAY. He died in 1439. He married CATHERINE STIRLING.

Generation 6

8. **DAVID[6] LINDSAY** (Katherine[5] Stewart, John[5] Stewart, James[2] Stewart, Walter Alexander[1] Stewart) was born in 1410 in Crawford, Lanarkshire, Scotland. He died on 17 Jan 1446 in Angusshire, Scotland, Battle of Aberbrothock.. He married **MARGORIE OGILVIE**. She was born in 1410. She died in 1476.

Notes for David Lindsay:
Lord, 3rd Earl of Crawford. Sheriff of Aberdeen, died in Battle of Aberbrothock 7 January 1445/46.

David Lindsay and Margorie Ogilvie had the following child:

10. i. WALTER[7] LINDSAY was born in 1445 in Auchtermuchty, Fife, Scotland. He died in 1517 in Finhaven Castle, Angusshire, Scotland. He married (1) ISABEL LIVINGSTON. She was born in 1432. She died on 15 Jun 1509 in Perth, Perthshire, Scotland. He married (2) JEAN JANET JEANETTE SINCLAIR/ST. CLAIR. He married (3) SOPHIA LIVINGSTON.

9. **ALEXANDER[6] LINDSAY** (Katherine[5] Stewart, John[5] Stewart, James[2] Stewart, Walter Alexander[1] Stewart, David, Alexander, David). He died in 1439. He married **CATHERINE STIRLING**.

Generation 6 (cont.)

Notes for Alexander Lindsay:
Sir knighted at the cornation of King James May 21, 1424, Lord, 1st Earl of Crawford. A Genealogical and Heritage History of the Peerage and Baronetage.

Acquired lands at Edzell and Glenesk through marriage to Catherine Stirling in 1358.

Notes for Catherine Stirling:
The Stirlings of Glenesk are said to have been descendants of Henry de Strevelin, youngest son of David, Earl of Huntington, the brother of King William, the Lion. The Stirlings acquired Glenesk at a very early date and the last male proprietor of the name was Sir John de Striveling, whose daughter and heiress, married in 1365, Sir Alexander Lindsay, third son of Sir David Lindsay of Crawford. Sir David Lindsay, who was created Earl of Crawford in 1398, was the eldest child of Sir Alexander Lindsay and Catherine Stirling. Lord Lindsay says that "The cognisance of the Stirlins of Glenesk as three stars, in common with the house of De Moravia and othern northern families (*Lives of the Lindsays,* Vol. I, p. 51) (the Stirlings being even sometimes being territorially De Movaria . . . By way of a family differences, in right of his descent from Ctherine de Striveline, mother of David, first Earl of Crawford, the daughter and heiress of Sir Joh Striveline of Glenesk (head of an ancient and powerful family, whose arms consiste solely of stars), he added the stars to his Coat. The stars are still visibly sculptured upon the prominent parts of the old Castle of Edzell, which lay within the barony of Glenesk. Hence by Scottish practice, they

Generation 6 (cont.)

became what were termed the 'feudal arms' of the Barony, which were also derived from the first tenants in capite or possession--in this stance, undoubtedly the Strivelynes."

Tradition gives another account of the succession of the Lindsays to Glenesk. It is said that the last Sir John Striveline of Glenesk had a son and a daughter. "They were left orphans and the former, small of stature and greatly deformed in body as familiarily known by the diminitive cognomen of 'Jackie Stirlin.' Although physically defective, he enjoyed excellent health and was neither impervious to the softer feelings of humanity nor too unseemly for the kindly eyes of women, by one of whom, the lovely daughter of a neighboring baron, his offer of marriage was accepted.

"This was altogether contrary to the wishes and expectations of his sister and her lover, the gallant Sir Alexander Lindsay, and all remonstrances having failed to prevent the nuptials, they laid a deep and heartless scheme for his overthrow, and one evening while taking an airing alone in the wooded defile, he was pounced upon by a masked assailant and summarily dispatchd at a point still pointed out a little to the north of the Castle." *(Land of the Lindsays, p. 26).*

Part of the old Castle of Edzell, once the residence of the Stirlings of Glenesk, is called "Stirling Tower" and is believed to have been erected by them.

Generation 6 (cont.)

Alexander Lindsay and Catherine Stirling had the following child:

8. i. DAVID[6] LINDSAY was born in 1410 in Crawford, Lanarkshire, Scotland. He died on 17 Jan 1446 in Angusshire, Scotland, Battle of Aberbrothock.. He married MARGORIE OGILVIE. She was born in 1410. She died in 1476.

Generation 7

10. **WALTER[7] LINDSAY** (David[6], Katherine[5] Stewart, John[5] Stewart, James[2] Stewart, Walter Alexander[1] Stewart) was born in 1445 in Auchtermuchty, Fife, Scotland. He died in 1517 in Finhaven Castle, Angusshire, Scotland. He married (1) **ISABEL LIVINGSTON**. She was born in 1432. She died on 15 Jun 1509 in Perth, Perthshire, Scotland. He married (2) **JEAN JANET JEANETTE SINCLAIR/ST. CLAIR**. He married (3) **SOPHIA LIVINGSTON**.

Notes for Walter Lindsay:
Married in 1470, died 1475. See "Wood's Douglas's Peerage of Scotland, " I, 164, 376. "Tutor" to Earl David. Earl of Crawford. Third son of Alexander 2nd Earl of Crawford. Magna Charta Barons and their American Descendants; the Descent of General Robert Edward Lee from Robert The Bruce, of Scotland.

Notes for Isabel Livingston:
Also name given as Sophia.

Walter Lindsay and Isabel Livingston had the

Generation 7 (cont.)

following child:

11. i. DAVID[8] LINDSAY was born in 1455 in Edzell, Aberdeenshire, Scotland. He died on 27 Nov 1528 in Auchtermonzie, Scotland. He married (1) ELIZABETH SPENCE. She died in 1532. He married (2) AGNES OGILVY. He married (3) KATHERINE FOTHERINGTON. She was born in 1460. She died in 1488 in Somme, Picardie, France.

Walter Lindsay and Jean Janet Jeanette Sinclair/St. Clair had the following children:

ii. ELISABETH LINDSAY was born in 1505.

iii. SIBILLA LINDSAY was born in 1515.

iv. ISOBEL LINDSAY was born in 1526.

v. DAVID LINDSAY was born in 1527.

vi. ELIZABETH ALEXANDER LINDSAY was born in 1531.

Generation 8

11. **DAVID[8] LINDSAY** (Walter[7], David[6], Katherine[5] Stewart, John[5] Stewart, James[2] Stewart, Walter Alexander[1] Stewart) was born in 1455 in Edzell, Aberdeenshire, Scotland. He died on 27 Nov 1528 in Auchtermonzie, Scotland. He married (1) **ELIZABETH SPENCE**. She died in 1532. He married (2) **AGNES OGILVY**. He married (3) **KATHERINE FOTHERINGTON**. She was born in 1460. She died in 1488 in Somme, Picardie,

Generation 8 (cont.)

France.

Notes for David Lindsay:
Sir David Lindsay, of Beaufort and Edzell, a Member of Parliment, 1487, died in 1528. He married first, Katherine, daughter of Thomas Fotheringham of Powrie. The Lindsays were prominent in both England and Scotland from the late 11th century.

David Lindsay and Elizabeth Spence had the following child:

12. i. WALTER THOMAS[9] LINDSAY was born in 1480 in Edzell, Angus, Scotland. He died on 09 Sep 1513 in Battle of Flodden Field, Branxton, Northumberland, England. He married Elizabeth Erskine in 1500 in Edzell, Lanarkshire, Scotland. She was born in 1475 in Edzell, Angus, Scotland. She died in 1540 in Haddington, East Lothian, Scotland.

David Lindsay and Agnes Ogilvy had the following child:

12. i. WALTER THOMAS[9] LINDSAY was born in 1480 in Edzell, Angus, Scotland. He died on 09 Sep 1513 in Battle of Flodden Field, Branxton, Northumberland, England. He married Elizabeth Erskine in 1500 in Edzell, Lanarkshire, Scotland. She was born in 1475 in Edzell, Angus, Scotland. She died in 1540 in Haddington, East

Generation 8 (cont.)

Lothian, Scotland.

David Lindsay and Katherine Fotherington had the following children:

13. iii. RACHEL LINDSAY was born in 1563. She died on 02 Dec 1639 in Ross, Scotland. She married JOHN SPOTTISWOODE. He was born in 1565. He died on 17 Nov 1639 in London, England.

14. iv. WALTER LINDSAY. He died on 09 Sep 1513. He married ERSKINE.

v. ALEXANDER LINDSAY.

vi. DAVID LINDSAY.

Generation 9

12. **WALTER THOMAS^{9} LINDSAY** (David^{8}, Walter^{7}, David^{6}, Katherine^{5} Stewart, John^{5} Stewart, James^{2} Stewart, Walter Alexander^{1} Stewart) was born in 1480 in Edzell, Angus, Scotland. He died on 09 Sep 1513 in Battle of Flodden Field, Branxton, Northumberland, England. He married Elizabeth Erskine in 1500 in Edzell, Lanarkshire, Scotland. She was born in 1475 in Edzell, Angus, Scotland. She died in 1540 in Haddington, East Lothian, Scotland.

Walter Thomas Lindsay and Elizabeth Erskine had the following children:

i. BISHOP^{10} LINDSAY was born in 1505.

15. ii. ALEXANDER DAVID LINDSAY was born in 1508. He married (1) JANET GRAY. He

Generation 9 (cont.)

married (2) CATHERINE (CALDER) CAMPBELL.

16. iii. ROBERT LINDSAY was born in 1509.

17. iv. ALEXANDER DAVID LINDSAY was born in 1532 in Pittormie, Scotland. He married RACHEL (MATHERS) BARCLAY.

18. v. JOHN LINDSAY. He married JOAN STEWART.

13. **RACHEL LINDSAY** (David[8], Walter[7], David[6], Katherine[5] Stewart, John[5] Stewart, James[2] Stewart, Walter Alexander[1] Stewart) was born in 1563. She died on 02 Dec 1639 in Ross, Scotland. She married **JOHN SPOTTISWOODE**. He was born in 1565. He died on 17 Nov 1639 in London, England.

Notes for John Spottiswoode:
Archbishop of St. Andrews in 1615; Lord High Chancellor of Scotland, 1635. He crowned King Charles I, at Holyrood, in 1639. Buried by King's demand at Westminster Abbey (see Playfair's "British Family Antiquity," VIII, 805.

John Spottiswoode and Rachel Lindsay had the following child:

19. i. ROBERT SPOTTISWOODE was born in 1596 in Dunipace, Stirlingshire, Scotland. He died on 16 Jan 1646 in St. Andrews, Fife, Scotland. He married Bethia Morrison, daughter of Alexander Morrison and Eleanor Maule, in 1629. She was born in 1608. She died on 17 Nov 1639 in

Generation 9 (cont.)

Wedderburn Castle, Berwickshire, Scotland.

14. **WALTER[9] LINDSAY** (David[8], Walter[7], David[6], Katherine[5] Stewart, John[5] Stewart, James[2] Stewart, Walter Alexander[1] Stewart, David[8], Walter[7], David[6], David, Alexander, David). He died on 09 Sep 1513. He married **ERSKINE**.

Notes for Erskine:
"The Younger" of Edzell, was killed at the Battle of Flodden Field 9 September 1513.

Walter Lindsay and Erskine had the following children:

16. i. ROBERT[10] LINDSAY was born in 1509.

17. ii. ALEXANDER DAVID LINDSAY was born in 1532 in Pittormie, Scotland. He married RACHEL (MATHERS) BARCLAY.

18. iii. JOHN LINDSAY. He married JOAN STEWART.

Generation 10

15. **ALEXANDER DAVID[10] LINDSAY** (Walter Thomas[9], David[8], Walter[7], David[6], Katherine[5] Stewart, John[5] Stewart, James[2] Stewart, Walter Alexander[1] Stewart) was born in 1508. He married (1) **JANET GRAY**. He married (2) **CATHERINE (CALDER) CAMPBELL**.

Alexander David Lindsay and Catherine (Calder) Campbell had the following children:

20. i. DAVID ROSS[11] LINDSAY was born in 1532 in Pittormie. He died in 1613 in Leith, Edinburgh, Scotland. He married

Generation 10 (cont.)

(1) JONETA RAMSAY. He married (2) HELEN HARRESON.

ii. DAVID LINDSAY.

iii. JOHN LINDSAY.

16. **ROBERT^{10} LINDSAY** (Walter Thomas^{9}, David^{8}, Walter^{7}, David^{6}, Katherine^{5} Stewart, John^{5} Stewart, James^{2} Stewart, Walter Alexander^{1} Stewart) was born in 1509.

Robert Lindsay had the following child:

21. i. DAVID^{11} LINDSAY was born in 1531 in Halftoun, Puttorlie, Scotland. He died on 17 Dec 1613 in Annatland, Angusshire, Scotland.

17. **ALEXANDER DAVID^{10} LINDSAY** (Walter Thomas^{9}, David^{8}, Walter^{7}, David^{6}, Katherine^{5} Stewart, John^{5} Stewart, James^{2} Stewart, Walter Alexander^{1} Stewart) was born in 1532 in Pittormie, Scotland. He married **RACHEL (MATHERS) BARCLAY**.

Alexander David Lindsay and Rachel (Mathers) Barclay had the following children:

20. i. DAVID ROSS^{11} LINDSAY was born in 1532 in Pittormie. He died in 1613 in Leith, Edinburgh, Scotland. He married (1) JONETA RAMSAY. He married (2) HELEN HARRESON.

ii. DAVID LINDSAY.

iii. JOHN LINDSAY.

Generation 10 (cont.)

18. **JOHN[10] LINDSAY** (Walter Thomas[9], David[8], Walter[7], David[6], Katherine[5] Stewart, John[5] Stewart, James[2] Stewart, Walter Alexander[1] Stewart, Walter[9], David[8], Walter[7], David[6], David, Alexander, David). He married **JOAN STEWART**.

John Lindsay and Joan Stewart had the following children:

22. i. PATRICK[11] LINDSAY was born in 1526. He married ISABELLA PITCAIRN.

ii. JOHN LINDSAY. He died in 1563.

Notes for John Lindsay:
5th Lord Lindsay of the Byres (died 1563) was a Scottish judge.

19. **ROBERT SPOTTISWOODE** (Rachel Lindsay, David[8] Lindsay, Walter[7] Lindsay, David[6] Lindsay, Katherine[5] Stewart, John[5] Stewart, James[2] Stewart, Walter Alexander[1] Stewart) was born in 1596 in Dunipace, Stirlingshire, Scotland. He died on 16 Jan 1646 in St. Andrews, Fife, Scotland. He married Bethia Morrison, daughter of Alexander Morrison and Eleanor Maule, in 1629. She was born in 1608. She died on 17 Nov 1639 in Wedderburn Castle, Berwickshire, Scotland.

Notes for Robert Spottiswoode:
See the "Sottiswood Miscellany," 1844, Vol. I. He was a member of the Privy Council to James VI, of Scotland and was appointed by King Charles I. Lawyer, Knighted Sir, Beheaded, January 16, 1646.

Robert Spottiswoode and Bethia Morrison had the following child:

Generation 10 (cont.)

i. ROBERT SPOTTISWOODE was born in 1637. He died in 1680.

Notes for Robert Spottiswoode:
Genealogy of the Spotswood Family in Scotland and Virginia.

Generation 11

20. **DAVID ROSS*11* LINDSAY** (Alexander David*10*, Walter Thomas*9*, David*8*, Walter*7*, David*6*, Katherine*5* Stewart, John*5* Stewart, James*2* Stewart, Walter Alexander*1* Stewart) was born in 1532 in Pittormie. He died in 1613 in Leith, Edinburgh, Scotland. He married (1) **JONETA RAMSAY**. He married (2) **HELEN HARRESON**.

Notes for David Ross Lindsay:
Bishop of Ross. Called Father of the Church. A man of great ablity and deep learning. Having traveled in France and Switzerland, he imbibed Reformation principles and was one of the twelve Reformation ministers nominated in July 1560, to the "chief places in Scotland," the town of Leith being assigned to him. He was present at the first General Assembly on 20 December 1560, and his name occurs in 50 of the suceeding 73 Assemblies. He visited John Knox on his deathbed in 1572, and at Knox's request, went to the castle of Edinburgh to warn Sir William Kirkcaldy of Grange that unless he gave it up, he "should be brought down over the walls of it with shame, and hung against the sun" by his political enemies. After his unsuccessful mission, he interceded for Kirkcaldy after his condemnation, attended him on the scafford

Generation 11 (cont.)

after intercession failed, and witnessed the literal fufillment of the doom pronounced by Knox. David Lindsay filled a conspicious place in affairs of Church and State, he was "the minister whom the Court liked best."

He accompanied King James to Denmark as Chaplain, and on 23 November 1589 officiated at his wedding to Anne of Denmark at Upsala. He was the only minister of note who had prayers for the beautiful and unhappy Mary, Queen of Scots, at the time of her execution. At the baptism of Prince Henry at Stirling in 1594, he preached to the Ambassadors in French; he also baptized Princess Margaret and Prince Charles (who was to become King).

The testament dative and inventory of the goods, gear, sums of money and debt pertaining to "umquhile Reverend fathyr in God, David, Bishop of Ross, Indweller in Leith the tyme of his deceas, quha deceist in Leith upon the xiiij day of August, the yeire of God, 1613 yeirs," list his son Sir Jerome Lindsay, one of the Comissioners of Edinburgh, as executor dative of the will, and several debts due the late Bishop were listed. Thia was confirmed by the Commissary of Edinburgh on 17 December 1613. *Register of Edinburgh Testamentsl,* CC8/8/56; Scottish Records Office, CC8/8/17.

David Ross Lindsay and Joneta Ramsay had the following child:

i. JEROME[12] LINDSAY was born in 1562. He died in 1642. He married

Generation 11 (cont.)

MARGARET COLVILLE.

Notes for Jerome Lindsay:
Lord Lyon

21. **DAVID[11] LINDSAY** (Rachel, David[8], Walter[7], David[6], Katherine[5] Stewart, John[5] Stewart, James[2] Stewart, Walter Alexander[1] Stewart) was born in 1531 in Halftoun, Puttorlie, Scotland. He died on 17 Dec 1613 in Annatland, Angusshire, Scotland.

Notes for David Lindsay:
DD, Bishop of Ross, 1600.

David Lindsay had the following child:

13. i. RACHEL LINDSAY was born in 1563. She died on 02 Dec 1639 in Ross, Scotland. She married JOHN SPOTTISWOODE. He was born in 1565. He died on 17 Nov 1639 in London, England.

22. **PATRICK[11] LINDSAY** (John[10], Walter Thomas[9], David[8], Walter[7], David[6], Katherine[5] Stewart, John[5] Stewart, James[2] Stewart, Walter Alexander[1] Stewart) was born in 1526. He married **ISABELLA PITCAIRN**.

Notes for Patrick Lindsay:
Of Kirkforthar 4th Lord of the Byres. Lindsay was said to have advised the nobles of Scotland to fight at Flodden on 9 September 1513 but sent James IV home. In Pittscottie's story, Lindsay compared the forthcoming encounter to a wager of a gold rose-noble against a bent halfpenny.

Generation 11 (cont.)

He was a reputed advisor of James IV of Scotland, and appointed in December, 1513, counsellor to Margaret Tudor. The arrangement did not last as Margaret married the Earl of Angus and John Stewart, Duke of Albany became regent. In May 1524 Regent Albany appointed Patrick and his son and grandson joint Sheriffs of Fife. Alexander Crawford Lindsay, "Lives of the Lindsays", or "A memoir of the houses of Crawford and Balcarres", vol. 1 (1849), pp. 183-85, 188-9. Macdougall, Norman,"James III", John Donald (1982), p. 283, footnote 19.

Patrick Lindsay and Isabella Pitcairn had the following children:

23. i. JAMES[12] LINDSAY was born in 1584 in Melrose Melrose, Roxburgh, Scotland. He died on 11 Oct 1623 in Scotland. He married KATHEREIN GEMMILL.

ii. JEAN LINDSAY.

24. iii. JOHN LINDSAY.

Generation 12

23. **JAMES[12] LINDSAY** (Patrick[11], John[10], Walter Thomas[9], David[8], Walter[7], David[6], Katherine[5] Stewart, John[5] Stewart, James[2] Stewart, Walter Alexander[1] Stewart) was born in 1584 in Melrose Melrose, Roxburgh, Scotland. He died on 11 Oct 1623 in Scotland. He married **KATHEREIN GEMMILL**.

James Lindsay and Katherein Gemmill had the

Generation 12 (cont.)

following child:

25. i. ALEXANDER^{13} LINDSAY was born in 1610 in Glasgow, Lanarkshire, Scotland. He died about 1718 in Annatland, Angushire Co., Scotland. He married ISOBELL WATSON. She was born in 1613.

24. **JOHN^{12} LINDSAY** (Patrick^{11}, John^{10}, Walter Thomas^{9}, David^{8}, Walter^{7}, David^{6}, Katherine^{5} Stewart, John^{5} Stewart, James^{2} Stewart, Walter Alexander^{1} Stewart, Patrick^{11}, John^{10}, Walter^{9}, David^{8}, Walter^{7}, David^{6}, David, Alexander, David).

Notes for John Lindsay:
Sir John, Master of Lindsay.

John Lindsay had the following child:

i. JOHN^{13} LINDSAY.

Generation 13

25. **ALEXANDER^{13} LINDSAY** (James^{12}, Patrick^{11}, John^{10}, Walter Thomas^{9}, David^{8}, Walter^{7}, David^{6}, Katherine^{5} Stewart, John^{5} Stewart, James^{2} Stewart, Walter Alexander^{1} Stewart) was born in 1610 in Glasgow, Lanarkshire, Scotland. He died about 1718 in Annatland, Angushire Co., Scotland. He married **ISOBELL WATSON**. She was born in 1613.

Notes for Alexander Lindsay:
Scotland, Selected Births and Baptisms, 1564-1950; Scotland, Select Marriages, 1561-1910; U.S. and Canada, Passenger and Immigration Lists, 1500s-

Generation 13 (cont.)

1900s.

Alexander Lindsay and Isobell Watson had the following child:

26. i. ALEXANDER II[14] LINDSAY was born on 08 Nov 1637 in Lanarkshire, Scotland. He died in 1664 in United States. He married Agnes Thomson Muir, daughter of William Muir and Katherine Henderson Murdoch, in 1663 in Virginia, United States. She was born in Ochiltree, Ayrshire, Scotland. She died in 1684 in Ayrshire, Scotland.

Generation 14

26. **ALEXANDER II[14] LINDSAY** (Alexander[13], James[12], Patrick[11], John[10], Walter Thomas[9], David[8], Walter[7], David[6], Katherine[5] Stewart, John[5] Stewart, James[2] Stewart, Walter Alexander[1] Stewart) was born on 08 Nov 1637 in Lanarkshire, Scotland. He died in 1664 in United States. He married Agnes Thomson Muir, daughter of William Muir and Katherine Henderson Murdoch, in 1663 in Virginia, United States. She was born in Ochiltree, Ayrshire, Scotland. She died in 1684 in Ayrshire, Scotland.

Notes for Alexander II Lindsay:
Arrived in Virginia in 1655, age 18. Belfast, Northern Ireland, The Belfast Newsletter Publication January 3, 1905 (Death January 2, 1905) (Birth, Marriage and Death Notices) 1738-1925.

Notes for Agnes Thomson Muir:

Generation 14 (cont.)

Ayrshire & Stirling: The commissariot record of Glasgow Register of testaments, 1547-1800.

Alexander II Lindsay and Agnes Thomson Muir had the following children:

27. i. ALEXANDER III[15] LINDSAY was born on 22 May 1664 in Glasgow, Lanarkshire, Scotland. He died after 1705 in United States. He married (1) JANET RALSTON on 12 Dec 1687 in Glasgow, Lanarkshire, Scotland. She was born in 1663. He married (2) ELIZABETH FARAH on 14 Aug 1690 in Holy Trinity Minories, London, England.

ii. JOHN LINDSAY.

iii. JAMES LINDSAY.

iv. MARTHA LINDSAY.

v. AGNES LINDSAY.

vi. ISOBEL LINDSAY.

Generation 15

27. **ALEXANDER III[15] LINDSAY** (Alexander II[14], Alexander[13], James[12], Patrick[11], John[10], Walter Thomas[9], David[8], Walter[7], David[6], Katherine[5] Stewart, John[5] Stewart, James[2] Stewart, Walter Alexander[1] Stewart) was born on 22 May 1664 in Glasgow, Lanarkshire, Scotland. He died after 1705 in United States. He married (1) **JANET RALSTON** on 12 Dec 1687 in Glasgow, Lanarkshire, Scotland. She was born in 1663. He married (2) **ELIZABETH FARAH** on 14 Aug

Generation 15 (cont.)

1690 in Holy Trinity Minories, London, England.

Alexander III Lindsay and Janet Ralston had the following children:

i. JOHN[16] LINDSAY was born in 1685.

28. ii. WILLIAM ALEXANDER MALCOLM LINDSAY was born on 16 Jan 1685 in Glasgow, Lanarkshire, Scotland. He died in 1735 in Pennyslvania. He married Janet McCallum, daughter of Neil McCallum and Janet Maxwell, on 24 Nov 1713 in Govan, Lanarkshire, Scotland. She was born on 11 May 1684. She died in 1759.

iii. ALEXANDER (IV) LINDSAY was born in 1688.

Alexander III Lindsay and Elizabeth Farah had the following children:

iv. GEORGE LINDSAY was born in 1691.

v. MARGARET LINDSAY was born in 1693.

vi. THOMAS LINDSAY was born in 1696.

vii. MARY LINDSAY was born in 1698.

viii. JANET LINDSAY was born in 1705.

ix. WILLIAM LINDSAY.

x. ROBERT LINDSAY.

Generation 16

Generation 16 (cont.)

28. **William Alexander Malcolm**[16] **Lindsay** (Alexander III[15], Alexander II[14], Alexander[13], James[12], Patrick[11], John[10], Walter Thomas[9], David[8], Walter[7], David[6], Katherine[5] Stewart, John[5] Stewart, James[2] Stewart, Walter Alexander[1] Stewart) was born on 16 Jan 1685 in Glasgow, Lanarkshire, Scotland. He died in 1735 in Pennyslvania. He married Janet McCallum, daughter of Neil McCallum and Janet Maxwell, on 24 Nov 1713 in Govan, Lanarkshire, Scotland. She was born on 11 May 1684. She died in 1759.

Notes for William Alexander Malcolm Lindsay:
Arrivals: 1719 New Hampshire; 1735 Philadelphia, Pennsylvania.

William Alexander Malcolm Lindsay and Janet McCallum had the following children:

- i. Andrew[17] Lindsay was born in 1716.
- ii. Robert Lindsay was born in 1718.
- 29. iii. James Lindsay was born on 26 Nov 1721 in Glasgow, Borony, Scotland. He died on 02 Nov 1820 in Ohio, Allegheny, Pennsylvania. He married Margaret Hamilton, daughter of James Hamilton and Jean Arneill, on 22 Oct 1747 in East Kilbride, Lanarkshire, Scotland. She was born in 1727 in Govan, Lanarkshire, Scotland (Christening: 06 Oct 1728). She died in 1788.

Generation 17

Generation 17 (cont.)

29. **JAMES[17] LINDSAY** (William Alexander Malcolm[16], Alexander III[15], Alexander II[14], Alexander[13], James[12], Patrick[11], John[10], Walter Thomas[9], David[8], Walter[7], David[6], Katherine[5] Stewart, John[5] Stewart, James[2] Stewart, Walter Alexander[1] Stewart) was born on 26 Nov 1721 in Glasgow, Borony, Scotland. He died on 02 Nov 1820 in Ohio, Allegheny, Pennsylvania. He married Margaret Hamilton, daughter of James Hamilton and Jean Arneill, on 22 Oct 1747 in East Kilbride, Lanarkshire, Scotland. She was born in 1727 in Govan, Lanarkshire, Scotland (Christening: 06 Oct 1728). She died in 1788.

Notes for James Lindsay:
Baptism: December 17, 1721, St. Sepulchre, London, England.
Arrival age 4 Pennsylvania 1725.
He entered the Revolutionary War army, and died in the service.

Residences: 1770 Nether Providence, Chester County, Pennsylvania; 1798-1820 Union, Fayette, Pennsylvania.

James Lindsay and Margaret Hamilton had the following children:

30. i. WILLIAM S.[18] LINDSEY was born on 28 Dec 1771 in Glasgow, Lanarkshire, Scotland. He died on 19 Feb 1837 in Pike, Knox County, Ohio. He married Catherine Leidy Reed-Hoffman, daughter of Jacob Bergy Reed and Magdalena Leidy, in 1792 in New

Generation 17 (cont.)

Britain Township,Bucks County, Pennsylvania.. She was born in 1770 in Philadelphia, Montgomery, Pennsylvania. She died in 1844 in Perrysville, Ashland, Ohio.

ii. JAMES LINDSEY was born in 1772 in Ohio, Allegheny, Pennsylvania.

iii. PASTELL LINDSEY was born in 1772 in Ohio, Allegheny, Pennsylvania.

Generation 18

30. **WILLIAM S.**[18] **LINDSEY** (James[17] Lindsay, William Alexander Malcolm[16] Lindsay, Alexander III[15] Lindsay, Alexander II[14] Lindsay, Alexander[13] Lindsay, James[12] Lindsay, Patrick[11] Lindsay, John[10] Lindsay, Walter Thomas[9] Lindsay, David[8] Lindsay, Walter[7] Lindsay, David[6] Lindsay, Katherine[5] Stewart, John[5] Stewart, James[2] Stewart, Walter Alexander[1] Stewart) was born on 28 Dec 1771 in Glasgow, Lanarkshire, Scotland. He died on 19 Feb 1837 in Pike, Knox County, Ohio. He married Catherine Leidy Reed-Hoffman, daughter of Jacob Bergy Reed and Magdalena Leidy, in 1792 in New Britain Township,Bucks County, Pennsylvania.. She was born in 1770 in Philadelphia, Montgomery, Pennsylvania. She died in 1844 in Perrysville, Ashland, Ohio.

Notes for William S. Lindsey:
Baptism: January 1, 1760, Glasgow, Lanarkshire, Scotland; Naturalization Declaration July 20, 1827, Pennsylvania; Residence 1820-1837, Pike, Knox

Generation 18 (cont.)

County, Ohio.

William S. Lindsey and Catherine Leidy Reed-Hoffman had the following children:

i. ELIZABETH[19] LINDSEY-KARIGER was born in 1789. She died in 1871.

ii. JACOB LINDSEY was born in 1795. He died in 1839.

iii. CATHARINE 'CATY' LINDSEY was born in 1796. She died in 1878.

iv. MARY E. LINDSEY-BUTLER was born in 1799. She died in 1870.

v. NANCY LINDSEY-VIRSE was born in 1800. She died in 1883.

vi. SARAH ELIZABETH LINDSEY was born in 1803. She died in 1893.

vii. EVE LINDSEY-MCGINLEY was born in 1806. She died in 1893.

viii. JOHN LINDSEY was born in 1810.

ix. BARBARA LINDSEY was born in 1811 in Stark County, Ohio. She died in 1838.

x. WILLIAM LINDSEY was born in Jul 1813 in Stark County, Ohio. He died (Twin to Susan).

31. xi. SUSAN LINDSEY-PHIFER was born on 13 Jul 1813 in Stark County, Ohio (Twin to William Lindsey). Susan died on 18 Nov 1876 in Loudon, Fayette, Illinois (Burial Mount Moriah Cemetery).

Generation 18 (cont.)

Susan married Cornelius B. Phifer on 17 Dec 1828 in Knox County, Ohio. He was born in 1804. He died in 1884.

Generation 19

31. **SUSAN[19] LINDSEY-PHIFER** (William S.[18] Lindsey, James[17] Lindsay, William Alexander Malcolm[16] Lindsay, Alexander III[15] Lindsay, Alexander II[14] Lindsay, Alexander[13] Lindsay, James[12] Lindsay, Patrick[11] Lindsay, John[10] Lindsay, Walter Thomas[9] Lindsay, David[8] Lindsay, Walter[7] Lindsay, David[6] Lindsay, Katherine[5] Stewart, John[5] Stewart, James[2] Stewart, Walter Alexander[1] Stewart) was born on 13 Jul 1813 in Stark County, Ohio (Twin to William Lindsey). Susan died on 18 Nov 1876 in Loudon, Fayette, Illinois (Burial Mount Moriah Cemetery). Susan married Cornelius B. Phifer on 17 Dec 1828 in Knox County, Ohio. He was born in 1804. He died in 1884.

Cornelius B. Phifer and Susan Lindsey-Phifer had the following children:

32. i. GEORGE WASHINGTON[20] PHIFER was born in 1829. He died in 1909. He married Ellen Townsend on 28 Nov 1852 in Effingham, Illinois, USA. She was born in 1828 in Effingham, Illinois. She died on 26 Nov 1910 in Bates County, Missouri.

ii. WILLIAM C. PHIFER was born in 1831. He died in 1912.

Generation 19 (cont.)

iii. LUCINDA PHIFER-MOORE was born in 1834. She died in 1915.

iv. EMELINE PHIFER-STAHL was born in 1836. She died in 1915.

v. RACHEL PHIFER-GRANT was born in 1838. She died in 1894.

vi. CHRISTINA ANN PHIFER-HOAR-HOSENEY was born in 1840. She died in 1874.

vii. MARY ELIZABETH PHIFER was born in 1842. She died in 1842.

viii. MARY "CATHERINE" PHIFER-TISH-SPROAT was born in 1848. She died in 1901.

ix. JAMES A. PHIFER was born in 1852. He died in 1914.

x. REBECCA ELLEN PHIFER-BYARD was born in 1852 (Twin to James A. Phifer). She died in 1927.

Generation 20

32. **GEORGE WASHINGTON**[20] **PHIFER** (Susan[19] Lindsey-Phifer, William S.[18] Lindsey, James[17] Lindsay, William Alexander Malcolm[16] Lindsay, Alexander III[15] Lindsay, Alexander II[14] Lindsay, Alexander[13] Lindsay, James[12] Lindsay, Patrick[11] Lindsay, John[10] Lindsay, Walter Thomas[9] Lindsay, David[8] Lindsay, Walter[7] Lindsay, David[6] Lindsay, Katherine[5] Stewart, John[5] Stewart, James[2] Stewart, Walter Alexander[1] Stewart) was born in 1829. He died in 1909. He married Ellen Townsend on 28 Nov 1852 in Effingham, Illinois, USA. She was born in 1828 in Effingham, Illinois. She

Generation 20 (cont.)

died on 26 Nov 1910 in Bates County, Missouri.

George Washington Phifer and Ellen Townsend had the following children:

33. i. CHRISTINA[21] PHIFER-EWING was born in 1853 in Effingham, Effingham, Illinois, USA. She died in 1928. She married HENRY HARVEY EWING. He was born on 31 Mar 1848 in Wood, Virginia. He died on 10 Mar 1942 in Deer Creek, Bates, Missouri, USA.

ii. WILLIAM A. OR URIAH PHIFER was born in 1858. He died in 1945.

iii. FLORA E. PHIFER-STUBBLEFIELD was born in 1861. She died in 1943 in Bates County, Missouri.

iv. HANNAH PHIFER was born in 1863. She died in 1888 in Bates County, Missouri.

v. FANNY PHIFER was born in 1864.

vi. LEWIS PHIFER was born in 1865. He died in 1865.

vii. MARY ANGELINE PHIFER-HOYT was born in 1868. She died in 1949 in Bates County, Missouri.

viii. GEORGE W. PHIFER JR. was born in 1870. He died in 1965.

ix. LAURA LILLIAN PHIFER-EWING was born in 1872 in Bates County, Missouri. She died in 1966 in California.

Generation 21

33. **CHRISTINA[21] PHIFER-EWING** (George Washington[20] Phifer, Susan[19] Lindsey-Phifer, William S.[18] Lindsey, James[17] Lindsay, William Alexander Malcolm[16] Lindsay, Alexander III[15] Lindsay, Alexander II[14] Lindsay, Alexander[13] Lindsay, James[12] Lindsay, Patrick[11] Lindsay, John[10] Lindsay, Walter Thomas[9] Lindsay, David[8] Lindsay, Walter[7] Lindsay, David[6] Lindsay, Katherine[5] Stewart, John[5] Stewart, James[2] Stewart, Walter Alexander[1] Stewart) was born in 1853 in Effingham, Effingham, Illinois, USA. She died in 1928. She married **HENRY HARVEY EWING**. He was born on 31 Mar 1848 in Wood, Virginia. He died on 10 Mar 1942 in Deer Creek, Bates, Missouri, USA.

Henry Harvey Ewing and Christina Phifer-Ewing had the following children:

34. i. LAURA ELLA[22] EWING was born on 14 Sep 1877 in Effingham, Effingham, Illinois, USA. She died on 29 Aug 1953 in Butler, Bates County, Missouri. She married (1) LEWIS ALVIN DURBIN on 11 Dec 1898 in Effingham, Effingham, Illinois, USA. He was born in 1877 in Effingham, Effingham, Illinois, USA. He died on 18 May 1938 in Adrian, Bates County, Missouri. She married an unknown spouse on 11 Dec 1898 in Altamont, Illinois.

ii. LILIAN FLORENCE EWING was born on 24 Dec 1882 in Moccasin, Effingham. She died in 1965 in Bates County, Missouri.

Generation 21 (cont.)

iii. MARY VIVIAN EWING was born on 26 Feb 1889 in Effingham, Illinois. She died in 1980 in California.

Generation 22

34. **LAURA ELLA**[22] **EWING** (Christina[21] Phifer-Ewing, George Washington[20] Phifer, Susan[19] Lindsey-Phifer, William S.[18] Lindsey, James[17] Lindsay, William Alexander Malcolm[16] Lindsay, Alexander III[15] Lindsay, Alexander II[14] Lindsay, Alexander[13] Lindsay, James[12] Lindsay, Patrick[11] Lindsay, John[10] Lindsay, Walter Thomas[9] Lindsay, David[8] Lindsay, Walter[7] Lindsay, David[6] Lindsay, Katherine[5] Stewart, John[5] Stewart, James[2] Stewart, Walter Alexander[1] Stewart) was born on 14 Sep 1877 in Effingham, Effingham, Illinois, USA. She died on 29 Aug 1953 in Butler, Bates County, Missouri. She married (1) **LEWIS ALVIN DURBIN** on 11 Dec 1898 in Effingham, Effingham, Illinois, USA. He was born in 1877 in Effingham, Effingham, Illinois, USA. He died on 18 May 1938 in Adrian, Bates County, Missouri. She married an unknown spouse on 11 Dec 1898 in Altamont, Illinois.

Laura Ella Ewing had the following child:

35. i. NELLIE[23] BARKLEY was born on 06 Aug 1900 in Cass County, Archie, Missouri. She died on 27 Oct 1948 in Shawnee, Bates County, Missouri.

Lewis Alvin Durbin and Laura Ella Ewing had the following children:

i. LESLIE ALVIN[23] DURBIN was born on 11 Oct 1908 in Bates County, Missouri.

Generation 22 (cont.)

He died on 27 Sep 1952 in Adrian, Bates County, Missouri.

ii. JESSE WILLIAM DURBIN was born in 1911 in Bates County, Missouri.

iii. UFA HENRY DURBIN.

Generation 23

35. **NELLIE[23] BARKLEY** (Laura Ella[22] Ewing, Christina[21] Phifer-Ewing, George Washington[20] Phifer, Susan[19] Lindsey-Phifer, William S.[18] Lindsey, James[17] Lindsay, William Alexander Malcolm[16] Lindsay, Alexander III[15] Lindsay, Alexander II[14] Lindsay, Alexander[13] Lindsay, James[12] Lindsay, Patrick[11] Lindsay, John[10] Lindsay, Walter Thomas[9] Lindsay, David[8] Lindsay, Walter[7] Lindsay, David[6] Lindsay, Katherine[5] Stewart, John[5] Stewart, James[2] Stewart, Walter Alexander[1] Stewart) was born on 06 Aug 1900 in Cass County, Archie, Missouri. She died on 27 Oct 1948 in Shawnee, Bates County, Missouri.

Nellie Barkley had the following children:

i. MARVIN DARRELL DURBIN was born in 1924 in Bates County, Missouri. He died in 1992 in Seattle, Washinton.

ii. JACK CALVIN DURBIN was born on 23 Sep 1925 in Bates County, Missouri. He died in 2012 in Wichita, Sedgwick, Kansas, USA.

iii. LEONARD LEROY DURBIN was born on 20 Aug 1927 in Archie, Cass, Missouri. He died in 1995 in Butler, Bates

Generation 23 (cont.)

County, Missouri.

iv. BETTY JEWELL DURBIN was born on 02 Feb 1931 in Shawnee, Bates County, Missouri. She married WINFRED LEE CARSON SR..

v. DORIS MAY DURBIN was born on 11 Aug 1932 in Adrian, Missouri (Shawnee Twp, Bates County, Missouri). She died in Manvel, Brazoria, Texas (Ashes scattered, Happy, Texas). She married Ovid Maurice Wooley, son of Ovid Garlington Wooley and Mildred Maurine Walker, on 17 Feb 1952 in Wichita, Sedgwick, Kansas, USA (At home of brother Jack & Maedean.). He was born on 03 Jul 1933 in Happy, Texas. He died on 05 Nov 2004 in Caynon, Happy, Texas.

Notes for Doris May Durbin:
Cremated, ashes scattered on old home place, Happy, Texas.

vi. PEGGY JOYCE DURBIN was born on 02 Jul 1936 in Shawnee, Bates County, Missouri. She married IRVIN LEE BEERY.

vii. CAROL JEAN DURBIN was born on 01 Jul 1940 in Shawnee, Bates County, Missouri. She married Arthur Bidner on 03 Mar 1962 in Kansas City, Missouri.

Generation 23 (cont.)

He was born on 17 Feb 1932 in Brooklyn, New York.

Descendants of David Lindsay

Generation 1

1. **DAVID[1] LINDSAY** . He married **KATHERINE STEWART**.

David Lindsay and Katherine Stewart had the following children:

2.	i.	DAVID[2] LINDSAY was born in 1410 in Crawford, Lanarkshire, Scotland. He died on 17 Jan 1446 in Angusshire, Scotland, Battle of Aberbrothock.. He married MARGORIE OGILVIE. She was born in 1410. She died in 1476.
3.	ii.	ALEXANDER LINDSAY. He died in 1439. He married CATHERINE STIRLING.

Generation 2

2. **DAVID[2] LINDSAY** (David[1]) was born in 1410 in Crawford, Lanarkshire, Scotland. He died on 17 Jan 1446 in Angusshire, Scotland, Battle of Aberbrothock.. He married **MARGORIE OGILVIE**. She was born in 1410. She died in 1476.

Notes for David Lindsay:
Lord, 3rd Earl of Crawford. Sheriff of Aberdeen, died in Battle of Aberbrothock 7 January 1445/46.

David Lindsay and Margorie Ogilvie had the following child:

4.	i.	WALTER[3] LINDSAY was born in 1445 in Auchtermuchty, Fife, Scotland. He died in 1517 in Finhaven Castle,

Generation 2 (cont.)

Angusshire, Scotland. He married (1) ISABEL LIVINGSTON. She was born in 1432. She died on 15 Jun 1509 in Perth, Perthshire, Scotland. He married (2) JEAN JANET JEANETTE SINCLAIR/ST. CLAIR. He married (3) SOPHIA LIVINGSTON.

3. **ALEXANDER**[2] **LINDSAY** (David[1]). He died in 1439. He married **CATHERINE STIRLING**.

Notes for Alexander Lindsay:
Sir knighted at the cornation of King James May 21, 1424, Lord, 1st Earl of Crawford. A Genealogical and Heritage History of the Peerage and Baronetage.

Acquired lands at Edzell and Glenesk through marriage to Catherine Stirling in 1358.

Notes for Catherine Stirling:
The Stirlings of Glenesk are said to have been descendants of Henry de Strevelin, youngest son of David, Earl of Huntington, the brother of King William, the Lion. The Stirlings acquired Glenesk at a very early date and the last male proprietor of the name was Sir John de Striveling, whose daughter and heiress, married in 1365, Sir Alexander Lindsay, third son of Sir David Lindsay of Crawford. Sir David Lindsay, who was created Earl of Crawford in 1398, was the eldest child of Sir Alexander Lindsay and Catherine Stirling. Lord Lindsay says that "The cognisance of the

Generation 2 (cont.)

Stirlins of Glenesk as three stars, in common with the house of De Moravia and othern northern families (*Lives of the Lindsays,* Vol. I, p. 51) (the Stirlings being even sometimes being territorially De Movaria . . . By way of a family differences, in right of his descent from Ctherine de Striveline, mother of David, first Earl of Crawford, the daughter and heiress of Sir Joh Striveline of Glenesk (head of an ancient and powerful family, whose arms consiste solely of stars), he added the stars to his Coat. The stars are still visibly sculptured upon the prominent parts of the old Castle of Edzell, which lay within the barony of Glenesk. Hence by Scottish practice, they became what were termed the 'feudal arms' of the Barony, which were also derived from the first tenants in capite or possession--in this stance, undoubtedly the Strivelynes."

Tradition gives another account of the succession of the Lindsays to Glenesk. It is said that the last Sir John Striveline of Glenesk had a son and a daughter. "They were left orphans and the former, small of stature and greatly deformed in body as familiarily known by the diminitive cognomen of 'Jackie Stirlin.' Although physically defective, he enjoyed excellent health and was neither impervious to the softer feelings of humanity nor too unseemly for the kindly eyes of women, by one of whom, the lovely daughter of a neighboring baron, his offer of marriage was accepted.

Generation 2 (cont.)

"This was altogether contrary to the wishes and expectations of his sister and her lover, the gallant Sir Alexander Lindsay, and all remonstrances having failed to prevent the nuptials, they laid a deep and heartless scheme for his overthrow, and one evening while taking an airing alone in the wooded defile, he was pounced upon by a masked assailant and summarily dispatchd at a point still pointed out a little to the north of the Castle." (*Land of the Lindsays, p. 26).*

Part of the old Castle of Edzell, once the residence of the Stirlings of Glenesk, is called "Stirling Tower" and is believed to have been erected by them.

Alexander Lindsay and Catherine Stirling had the following child:

2. i. DAVID[2] LINDSAY was born in 1410 in Crawford, Lanarkshire, Scotland. He died on 17 Jan 1446 in Angusshire, Scotland, Battle of Aberbrothock.. He married MARGORIE OGILVIE. She was born in 1410. She died in 1476.

Generation 3

4. **WALTER[3] LINDSAY** (David[2], David[1]) was born in 1445 in Auchtermuchty, Fife, Scotland. He died in 1517 in Finhaven Castle, Angusshire, Scotland. He married (1) **ISABEL LIVINGSTON** . She was born in

Generation 3 (cont.)

1432. She died on 15 Jun 1509 in Perth, Perthshire, Scotland. He married (2) **JEAN JANET JEANETTE SINCLAIR/ST. CLAIR**. He married (3) **SOPHIA LIVINGSTON**.

Notes for Walter Lindsay:
Married in 1470, died 1475. See "Wood's Douglas's Peerage of Scotland, " I, 164, 376. "Tutor" to Earl David. Earl of Crawford. Third son of Alexander 2nd Earl of Crawford. Magna Charta Barons and their American Descendants; the Descent of General Robert Edward Lee from Robert The Bruce, of Scotland.

Notes for Isabel Livingston:
Also name given as Sophia.

Walter Lindsay and Isabel Livingston had the following child:

5. i. DAVID[4] LINDSAY was born in 1455 in Edzell, Aberdeenshire, Scotland. He died on 27 Nov 1528 in Auchtermonzie, Scotland. He married (1) ELIZABETH SPENCE. She died in 1532. He married (2) AGNES OGILVY. He married (3) KATHERINE FOTHERINGTON. She was born in 1460. She died in 1488 in Somme, Picardie, France.

Walter Lindsay and Jean Janet Jeanette Sinclair/St. Clair had the following children:

Generation 3 (cont.)

ii. ELISABETH LINDSAY was born in 1505.

iii. SIBILLA LINDSAY was born in 1515.

iv. ISOBEL LINDSAY was born in 1526.

v. DAVID LINDSAY was born in 1527.

vi. ELIZABETH ALEXANDER LINDSAY was born in 1531.

Generation 4

5. **DAVID[4] LINDSAY** (Walter[3], David[2], David[1]) was born in 1455 in Edzell, Aberdeenshire, Scotland. He died on 27 Nov 1528 in Auchtermonzie, Scotland. He married (1) **ELIZABETH SPENCE**. She died in 1532. He married (2) **AGNES OGILVY**. He married (3) **KATHERINE FOTHERINGTON**. She was born in 1460. She died in 1488 in Somme, Picardie, France.

Notes for David Lindsay:
Sir David Lindsay, of Beaufort and Edzell, a Member of Parliment, 1487, died in 1528. He married first, Katherine, daughter of Thomas Fotheringham of Powrie. The Lindsays were prominent in both England and Scotland from the late 11th century.

David Lindsay and Elizabeth Spence had the following child:

6. i. WALTER THOMAS[5] LINDSAY was born in 1480 in Edzell, Angus, Scotland.

Generation 4 (cont.)

He died on 09 Sep 1513 in Battle of Flodden Field, Branxton, Northumberland, England. He married Elizabeth Erskine in 1500 in Edzell, Lanarkshire, Scotland. She was born in 1475 in Edzell, Angus, Scotland. She died in 1540 in Haddington, East Lothian, Scotland.

David Lindsay and Agnes Ogilvy had the following child:

6. i. WALTER THOMAS[5] LINDSAY was born in 1480 in Edzell, Angus, Scotland. He died on 09 Sep 1513 in Battle of Flodden Field, Branxton, Northumberland, England. He married Elizabeth Erskine in 1500 in Edzell, Lanarkshire, Scotland. She was born in 1475 in Edzell, Angus, Scotland. She died in 1540 in Haddington, East Lothian, Scotland.

David Lindsay and Katherine Fotherington had the following children:

7. iii. RACHEL LINDSAY was born in 1563. She died on 02 Dec 1639 in Ross, Scotland. She married JOHN SPOTTISWOODE. He was born in 1565. He died on 17 Nov 1639 in London, England.

Generation 4 (cont.)

8. iv. WALTER LINDSAY. He died on 09 Sep 1513. He married ERSKINE.

v. ALEXANDER LINDSAY.

vi. DAVID LINDSAY.

Generation 5

6. **WALTER THOMAS[5] LINDSAY** (David[4], Walter[3], David[2], David[1]) was born in 1480 in Edzell, Angus, Scotland. He died on 09 Sep 1513 in Battle of Flodden Field, Branxton, Northumberland, England. He married Elizabeth Erskine in 1500 in Edzell, Lanarkshire, Scotland. She was born in 1475 in Edzell, Angus, Scotland. She died in 1540 in Haddington, East Lothian, Scotland.

Walter Thomas Lindsay and Elizabeth Erskine had the following children:

i. BISHOP[6] LINDSAY was born in 1505.

9. ii. ALEXANDER DAVID LINDSAY was born in 1508. He married (1) JANET GRAY. He married (2) CATHERINE (CALDER) CAMPBELL.

10. iii. ROBERT LINDSAY was born in 1509.

11. iv. ALEXANDER DAVID LINDSAY was born in 1532 in Pittormie, Scotland. He married RACHEL (MATHERS) BARCLAY.

12. v. JOHN LINDSAY. He married JOAN STEWART.

Generation 5 (cont.)

7. **RACHEL LINDSAY** (David[4], Walter[3], David[2], David[1]) was born in 1563. She died on 02 Dec 1639 in Ross, Scotland. She married **JOHN SPOTTISWOODE**. He was born in 1565. He died on 17 Nov 1639 in London, England.

   Notes for John Spottiswoode:
   Archbishop of St. Andrews in 1615; Lord High Chancellor of Scotland, 1635. He crowned King Charles I, at Holyrood, in 1639. Buried by King's demand at Westminster Abbey (see Playfair's "British Family Antiquity," VIII, 805.

   John Spottiswoode and Rachel Lindsay had the following child:

   13. i. ROBERT SPOTTISWOODE was born in 1596 in Dunipace, Stirlingshire, Scotland. He died on 16 Jan 1646 in St. Andrews, Fife, Scotland. He married Bethia Morrison, daughter of Alexander Morrison and Eleanor Maule, in 1629. She was born in 1608. She died on 17 Nov 1639 in Wedderburn Castle, Berwickshire, Scotland.

8. **WALTER[5] LINDSAY** (David[4], Walter[3], David[2], David[1]). He died on 09 Sep 1513. He married **ERSKINE**.

   Notes for Erskine:
   "The Younger" of Edzell, was killed at the Battle of Flodden Field 9 September 1513.

Generation 5 (cont.)

Walter Lindsay and Erskine had the following children:

10. i. ROBERT[6] LINDSAY was born in 1509.

11. ii. ALEXANDER DAVID LINDSAY was born in 1532 in Pittormie, Scotland. He married RACHEL (MATHERS) BARCLAY.

12. iii. JOHN LINDSAY. He married JOAN STEWART.

Generation 6

9. **ALEXANDER DAVID[6] LINDSAY** (Walter Thomas[5], David[4], Walter[3], David[2], David[1]) was born in 1508. He married (1) **JANET GRAY**. He married (2) **CATHERINE (CALDER) CAMPBELL**.

Alexander David Lindsay and Catherine (Calder) Campbell had the following children:

14. i. DAVID ROSS[7] LINDSAY was born in 1532 in Pittormie. He died in 1613 in Leith, Edinburgh, Scotland. He married (1) JONETA RAMSAY. He married (2) HELEN HARRESON.

ii. DAVID LINDSAY.

iii. JOHN LINDSAY.

10. **ROBERT[6] LINDSAY** (Walter Thomas[5], David[4], Walter[3], David[2], David[1]) was born in 1509.

Robert Lindsay had the following child:

Generation 6 (cont.)

15. i. DAVID[7] LINDSAY was born in 1531 in Halftoun, Puttorlie, Scotland. He died on 17 Dec 1613 in Annatland, Angusshire, Scotland.

11. **ALEXANDER DAVID[6] LINDSAY** (Walter Thomas[5], David[4], Walter[3], David[2], David[1]) was born in 1532 in Pittormie, Scotland. He married **RACHEL (MATHERS) BARCLAY**.

Alexander David Lindsay and Rachel (Mathers) Barclay had the following children:

14. i. DAVID ROSS[7] LINDSAY was born in 1532 in Pittormie. He died in 1613 in Leith, Edinburgh, Scotland. He married (1) JONETA RAMSAY. He married (2) HELEN HARRESON.

ii. DAVID LINDSAY.

iii. JOHN LINDSAY.

12. **JOHN[6] LINDSAY** (Walter Thomas[5], David[4], Walter[3], David[2], David[1], Walter[5], David[4], Walter[3], David[2], David[1]). He married **JOAN STEWART**.

John Lindsay and Joan Stewart had the following children:

16. i. PATRICK[7] LINDSAY was born in 1526. He married ISABELLA PITCAIRN.

ii. JOHN LINDSAY. He died in 1563.

Notes for John Lindsay:
5th Lord Lindsay of the Byres (died

Generation 6 (cont.)

1563) was a Scottish judge.

13. **ROBERT SPOTTISWOODE** (Rachel Lindsay, David[4] Lindsay, Walter[3] Lindsay, David[2] Lindsay, David[1] Lindsay) was born in 1596 in Dunipace, Stirlingshire, Scotland. He died on 16 Jan 1646 in St. Andrews, Fife, Scotland. He married Bethia Morrison, daughter of Alexander Morrison and Eleanor Maule, in 1629. She was born in 1608. She died on 17 Nov 1639 in Wedderburn Castle, Berwickshire, Scotland.

Notes for Robert Spottiswoode:
See the "Sottiswood Miscellany," 1844, Vol. I. He was a member of the Privy Council to James VI, of Scotland and was appointed by King Charles I. Lawyer, Knighted Sir, Beheaded, January 16, 1646.

Robert Spottiswoode and Bethia Morrison had the following child:

i. ROBERT SPOTTISWOODE was born in 1637. He died in 1680.

Notes for Robert Spottiswoode:
Genealogy of the Spotswood Family in Scotland and Virginia.

Generation 7

14. **DAVID ROSS[7] LINDSAY** (Alexander David[6], Walter Thomas[5], David[4], Walter[3], David[2], David[1]) was born in 1532 in Pittormie. He died in 1613 in Leith,

Generation 7 (cont.)

Edinburgh, Scotland. He married (1) **JONETA RAMSAY**. He married (2) **HELEN HARRESON**.

Notes for David Ross Lindsay:
Bishop of Ross. Called Father of the Church. A man of great ablity and deep learning. Having traveled in France and Switzerland, he imbibed Reformation principles and was one of the twelve Reformation ministers nominated in July 1560, to the "chief places in Scotland," the town of Leith being assigned to him. He was present at the first General Assembly on 20 December 1560, and his name occurs in 50 of the suceeding 73 Assemblies. He visited John Knox on his deathbed in 1572, and at Knox's request, went to the castle of Edinburgh to warn Sir William Kirkcaldy of Grange that unless he gave it up, he "should be brought down over the walls of it with shame, and hung against the sun" by his political enemies. After his unsuccessful mission, he interceded for Kirkcaldy after his condemnation, attended him on the scafford after intercession failed, and witnessed the literal fufillment of the doom pronounced by Knox. David Lindsay filled a conspicious place in affairs of Church and State, he was "the minister whom the Court liked best."

He accompanied King James to Denmark as Chaplain, and on 23 November 1589 officiated at his wedding to Anne of Denmark at Upsala. He was the only minister of note who had prayers for

Generation 7 (cont.)

the beautiful and unhappy Mary, Queen of Scots, at the time of her execution. At the baptism of Prince Henry at Stirling in 1594, he preached to the Ambassadors in French; he also baptized Princess Margaret and Prince Charles (who was to become King).

The testament dative and inventory of the goods, gear, sums of money and debt pertaining to "umquhile Reverend fathyr in God, David, Bishop of Ross, Indweller in Leith the tyme of his deceas, quha deceist in Leith upon the xiiij day of August, the yeire of God, 1613 yeirs," list his son Sir Jerome Lindsay, one of the Comissioners of Edinburgh, as executor dative of the will, and several debts due the late Bishop were listed. Thia was confirmed by the Commissary of Edinburgh on 17 December 1613.
Register of Edinburgh TestamentsI, CC8/8/56; Scottish Records Office, CC8/8/17.

David Ross Lindsay and Joneta Ramsay had the following child:

i. JEROME[8] LINDSAY was born in 1562. He died in 1642. He married MARGARET COLVILLE.

Notes for Jerome Lindsay:
Lord Lyon

15. **DAVID[7] LINDSAY** (Rachel, David[4], Walter[3], David[2], David[1]) was born in 1531 in Halftoun, Puttorlie,

Generation 7 (cont.)

Scotland. He died on 17 Dec 1613 in Annatland, Angusshire, Scotland.

Notes for David Lindsay:
DD, Bishop of Ross, 1600.

David Lindsay had the following child:

7. i. RACHEL LINDSAY was born in 1563. She died on 02 Dec 1639 in Ross, Scotland. She married JOHN SPOTTISWOODE. He was born in 1565. He died on 17 Nov 1639 in London, England.

16. **PATRICK[7] LINDSAY** (John[6], Walter Thomas[5], David[4], Walter[3], David[2], David[1]) was born in 1526. He married **ISABELLA PITCAIRN**.

Notes for Patrick Lindsay:
Of Kirkforthar 4th Lord of the Byres. Lindsay was said to have advised the nobles of Scotland to fight at Flodden on 9 September 1513 but sent James IV home. In Pittscottie's story, Lindsay compared the forthcoming encounter to a wager of a gold rose-noble against a bent halfpenny.

He was a reputed advisor of James IV of Scotland, and appointed in December, 1513, counsellor to Margaret Tudor. The arrangement did not last as Margaret married the Earl of Angus and John Stewart, Duke of Albany became regent. In May 1524 Regent Albany appointed Patrick and his son

Generation 7 (cont.)

and grandson joint Sheriffs of Fife. Alexander Crawford Lindsay, "Lives of the Lindsays", or "A memoir of the houses of Crawford and Balcarres", vol. 1 (1849), pp. 183-85, 188-9. Macdougall, Norman,"James III", John Donald (1982), p. 283, footnote 19.

Patrick Lindsay and Isabella Pitcairn had the following children:

17. i. JAMES[8] LINDSAY was born in 1584 in Melrose Melrose, Roxburgh, Scotland. He died on 11 Oct 1623 in Scotland. He married KATHEREIN GEMMILL.

ii. JEAN LINDSAY.

18. iii. JOHN LINDSAY.

Generation 8

17. **JAMES[8] LINDSAY** (Patrick[7], John[6], Walter Thomas[5], David[4], Walter[3], David[2], David[1]) was born in 1584 in Melrose Melrose, Roxburgh, Scotland. He died on 11 Oct 1623 in Scotland. He married **KATHEREIN GEMMILL**.

James Lindsay and Katherein Gemmill had the following child:

19. i. ALEXANDER[9] LINDSAY was born in 1610 in Glasgow, Lanarkshire, Scotland. He died about 1718 in Annatland, Angushire Co., Scotland.

Generation 8 (cont.)

He married ISOBELL WATSON. She was born in 1613.

18. **JOHN[8] LINDSAY** (Patrick[7], John[6], Walter Thomas[5], David[4], Walter[3], David[2], David[1], Patrick[7], John[6], Walter[5], David[4], Walter[3], David[2], David[1]).

Notes for John Lindsay:
Sir John, Master of Lindsay.

John Lindsay had the following child:

i. JOHN[9] LINDSAY.

Generation 9

19. **ALEXANDER[9] LINDSAY** (James[8], Patrick[7], John[6], Walter Thomas[5], David[4], Walter[3], David[2], David[1]) was born in 1610 in Glasgow, Lanarkshire, Scotland. He died about 1718 in Annatland, Angushire Co., Scotland. He married **ISOBELL WATSON**. She was born in 1613.

Notes for Alexander Lindsay:
Scotland, Selected Births and Baptisms, 1564-1950; Scotland, Select Marriages, 1561-1910; U.S. and Canada, Passenger and Immigration Lists, 1500s-1900s.

Alexander Lindsay and Isobell Watson had the following child:

20. i. ALEXANDER II[10] LINDSAY was born on 08 Nov 1637 in Lanarkshire, Scotland. He died in 1664 in United

Generation 9 (cont.)

States. He married Agnes Thomson Muir, daughter of William Muir and Katherine Henderson Murdoch, in 1663 in Virginia, United States. She was born in Ochiltree, Ayrshire, Scotland. She died in 1684 in Ayrshire, Scotland.

Generation 10

20. **ALEXANDER II[10] LINDSAY** (Alexander[9], James[8], Patrick[7], John[6], Walter Thomas[5], David[4], Walter[3], David[2], David[1]) was born on 08 Nov 1637 in Lanarkshire, Scotland. He died in 1664 in United States. He married Agnes Thomson Muir, daughter of William Muir and Katherine Henderson Murdoch, in 1663 in Virginia, United States. She was born in Ochiltree, Ayrshire, Scotland. She died in 1684 in Ayrshire, Scotland.

Notes for Alexander II Lindsay:
Arrived in Virginia in 1655, age 18. Belfast, Northern Ireland, The Belfast Newsletter Publication January 3, 1905 (Death January 2, 1905) (Birth, Marriage and Death Notices) 1738-1925.

Notes for Agnes Thomson Muir:
Ayrshire & Stirling: The commissariot record of Glasgow Register of testaments, 1547-1800.

Alexander II Lindsay and Agnes Thomson Muir had the following children:

Generation 10 (cont.)

21. i. ALEXANDER III[11] LINDSAY was born on 22 May 1664 in Glasgow, Lanarkshire, Scotland. He died after 1705 in United States. He married (1) JANET RALSTON on 12 Dec 1687 in Glasgow, Lanarkshire, Scotland. She was born in 1663. He married (2) ELIZABETH FARAH on 14 Aug 1690 in Holy Trinity Minories, London, England.

ii. JOHN LINDSAY.

iii. JAMES LINDSAY.

iv. MARTHA LINDSAY.

v. AGNES LINDSAY.

vi. ISOBEL LINDSAY.

Generation 11

21. **ALEXANDER III[11] LINDSAY** (Alexander II[10], Alexander[9], James[8], Patrick[7], John[6], Walter Thomas[5], David[4], Walter[3], David[2], David[1]) was born on 22 May 1664 in Glasgow, Lanarkshire, Scotland. He died after 1705 in United States. He married (1) **JANET RALSTON** on 12 Dec 1687 in Glasgow, Lanarkshire, Scotland. She was born in 1663. He married (2) **ELIZABETH FARAH** on 14 Aug 1690 in Holy Trinity Minories, London, England.

Alexander III Lindsay and Janet Ralston had the following children:

Generation 11 (cont.)

i. JOHN[12] LINDSAY was born in 1685.

22. ii. WILLIAM ALEXANDER MALCOLM LINDSAY was born on 16 Jan 1685 in Glasgow, Lanarkshire, Scotland. He died in 1735 in Pennyslvania. He married Janet McCallum, daughter of Neil McCallum and Janet Maxwell, on 24 Nov 1713 in Govan, Lanarkshire, Scotland. She was born on 11 May 1684. She died in 1759.

iii. ALEXANDER (IV) LINDSAY was born in 1688.

Alexander III Lindsay and Elizabeth Farah had the following children:

iv. GEORGE LINDSAY was born in 1691.

v. MARGARET LINDSAY was born in 1693.

vi. THOMAS LINDSAY was born in 1696.

vii. MARY LINDSAY was born in 1698.

viii. JANET LINDSAY was born in 1705.

ix. WILLIAM LINDSAY.

x. ROBERT LINDSAY.

Generation 12

22. **WILLIAM ALEXANDER MALCOLM[12] LINDSAY** (Alexander III[11], Alexander II[10], Alexander[9], James[8], Patrick[7], John[6], Walter Thomas[5], David[4],

Generation 12 (cont.)

Walter[3], David[2], David[1]) was born on 16 Jan 1685 in Glasgow, Lanarkshire, Scotland. He died in 1735 in Pennyslvania. He married Janet McCallum, daughter of Neil McCallum and Janet Maxwell, on 24 Nov 1713 in Govan, Lanarkshire, Scotland. She was born on 11 May 1684. She died in 1759.

Notes for William Alexander Malcolm Lindsay:
Arrivals: 1719 New Hampshire; 1735 Philadelphia, Pennsylvania.

William Alexander Malcolm Lindsay and Janet McCallum had the following children:

i. ANDREW[13] LINDSAY was born in 1716.

ii. ROBERT LINDSAY was born in 1718.

23. iii. JAMES LINDSAY was born on 26 Nov 1721 in Glasgow, Borony, Scotland. He died on 02 Nov 1820 in Ohio, Allegheny, Pennsylvania. He married Margaret Hamilton, daughter of James Hamilton and Jean Arneill, on 22 Oct 1747 in East Kilbride, Lanarkshire, Scotland. She was born in 1727 in Govan, Lanarkshire, Scotland (Christening: 06 Oct 1728). She died in 1788.

Generation 13

23. **JAMES[13] LINDSAY** (William Alexander Malcolm[12], Alexander III[11], Alexander II[10], Alexander[9],

Generation 13 (cont.)

James[8], Patrick[7], John[6], Walter Thomas[5], David[4], Walter[3], David[2], David[1]) was born on 26 Nov 1721 in Glasgow, Borony, Scotland. He died on 02 Nov 1820 in Ohio, Allegheny, Pennsylvania. He married Margaret Hamilton, daughter of James Hamilton and Jean Arneill, on 22 Oct 1747 in East Kilbride, Lanarkshire, Scotland. She was born in 1727 in Govan, Lanarkshire, Scotland (Christening: 06 Oct 1728). She died in 1788.

Notes for James Lindsay:
Baptism: December 17, 1721, St. Sepulchre, London, England.
Arrival age 4 Pennsylvania 1725.
He entered the Revolutionary War army, and died in the service.

Residences: 1770 Nether Providence, Chester County, Pennsylvania; 1798-1820 Union, Fayette, Pennsylvania.

James Lindsay and Margaret Hamilton had the following children:

24. i. WILLIAM S.[14] LINDSEY was born on 28 Dec 1771 in Glasgow, Lanarkshire, Scotland. He died on 19 Feb 1837 in Pike, Knox County, Ohio. He married Catherine Leidy Reed-Hoffman, daughter of Jacob Bergy Reed and Magdalena Leidy, in 1792 in New Britain Township,Bucks

Generation 13 (cont.)

County, Pennsylvania.. She was born in 1770 in Philadelphia, Montgomery, Pennsylvania. She died in 1844 in Perrysville, Ashland, Ohio.

ii. JAMES LINDSEY was born in 1772 in Ohio, Allegheny, Pennsylvania.

iii. PASTELL LINDSEY was born in 1772 in Ohio, Allegheny, Pennsylvania.

Generation 14

24. **WILLIAM S.**[14] **LINDSEY** (James[13] Lindsay, William Alexander Malcolm[12] Lindsay, Alexander III[11] Lindsay, Alexander II[10] Lindsay, Alexander[9] Lindsay, James[8] Lindsay, Patrick[7] Lindsay, John[6] Lindsay, Walter Thomas[5] Lindsay, David[4] Lindsay, Walter[3] Lindsay, David[2] Lindsay, David[1] Lindsay) was born on 28 Dec 1771 in Glasgow, Lanarkshire, Scotland. He died on 19 Feb 1837 in Pike, Knox County, Ohio. He married Catherine Leidy Reed-Hoffman, daughter of Jacob Bergy Reed and Magdalena Leidy, in 1792 in New Britain Township,Bucks County, Pennsylvania.. She was born in 1770 in Philadelphia, Montgomery, Pennsylvania. She died in 1844 in Perrysville, Ashland, Ohio.

Notes for William S. Lindsey:
Baptism: January 1, 1760, Glasgow, Lanarkshire, Scotland; Naturalization Declaration July 20, 1827,

Generation 14 (cont.)

Pennsylvania; Residence 1820-1837, Pike, Knox County, Ohio.

William S. Lindsey and Catherine Leidy Reed-Hoffman had the following children:

i. ELIZABETH[15] LINDSEY-KARIGER was born in 1789. She died in 1871.

ii. JACOB LINDSEY was born in 1795. He died in 1839.

iii. CATHARINE 'CATY' LINDSEY was born in 1796. She died in 1878.

iv. MARY E. LINDSEY-BUTLER was born in 1799. She died in 1870.

v. NANCY LINDSEY-VIRSE was born in 1800. She died in 1883.

vi. SARAH ELIZABETH LINDSEY was born in 1803. She died in 1893.

vii. EVE LINDSEY-MCGINLEY was born in 1806. She died in 1893.

viii. JOHN LINDSEY was born in 1810.

ix. BARBARA LINDSEY was born in 1811 in Stark County, Ohio. She died in 1838.

x. WILLIAM LINDSEY was born in Jul 1813 in Stark County, Ohio. He died (Twin to Susan).

25. xi. SUSAN LINDSEY-PHIFER was born on 13 Jul 1813 in Stark County, Ohio

Generation 14 (cont.)

(Twin to William Lindsey). Susan died on 18 Nov 1876 in Loudon, Fayette, Illinois (Burial Mount Moriah Cemetery). Susan married Cornelius B. Phifer on 17 Dec 1828 in Knox County, Ohio. He was born in 1804. He died in 1884.

Generation 15

25. **SUSAN[15] LINDSEY-PHIFER** (William S.[14] Lindsey, James[13] Lindsay, William Alexander Malcolm[12] Lindsay, Alexander III[11] Lindsay, Alexander II[10] Lindsay, Alexander[9] Lindsay, James[8] Lindsay, Patrick[7] Lindsay, John[6] Lindsay, Walter Thomas[5] Lindsay, David[4] Lindsay, Walter[3] Lindsay, David[2] Lindsay, David[1] Lindsay) was born on 13 Jul 1813 in Stark County, Ohio (Twin to William Lindsey). Susan died on 18 Nov 1876 in Loudon, Fayette, Illinois (Burial Mount Moriah Cemetery). Susan married Cornelius B. Phifer on 17 Dec 1828 in Knox County, Ohio. He was born in 1804. He died in 1884.

Cornelius B. Phifer and Susan Lindsey-Phifer had the following children:

26. i. GEORGE WASHINGTON[16] PHIFER was born in 1829. He died in 1909. He married Ellen Townsend on 28 Nov 1852 in Effingham, Illinois, USA. She was born in 1828 in Effingham, Illinois. She died on 26 Nov 1910 in

Generation 15 (cont.)

Bates County, Missouri.

ii. WILLIAM C. PHIFER was born in 1831. He died in 1912.

iii. LUCINDA PHIFER-MOORE was born in 1834. She died in 1915.

iv. EMELINE PHIFER-STAHL was born in 1836. She died in 1915.

v. RACHEL PHIFER-GRANT was born in 1838. She died in 1894.

vi. CHRISTINA ANN PHIFER-HOAR-HOSENEY was born in 1840. She died in 1874.

vii. MARY ELIZABETH PHIFER was born in 1842. She died in 1842.

viii. MARY "CATHERINE" PHIFER-TISH-SPROAT was born in 1848. She died in 1901.

ix. JAMES A. PHIFER was born in 1852. He died in 1914.

x. REBECCA ELLEN PHIFER-BYARD was born in 1852 (Twin to James A. Phifer). She died in 1927.

Generation 16

26. **GEORGE WASHINGTON** [16] **PHIFER** (Susan[15] Lindsey-Phifer, William S.[14] Lindsey, James[13] Lindsay, William Alexander Malcolm[12] Lindsay, Alexander III[11] Lindsay, Alexander II[10] Lindsay, Alexander[9]

Generation 16 (cont.)

Lindsay, James[8] Lindsay, Patrick[7] Lindsay, John[6] Lindsay, Walter Thomas[5] Lindsay, David[4] Lindsay, Walter[3] Lindsay, David[2] Lindsay, David[1] Lindsay) was born in 1829. He died in 1909. He married Ellen Townsend on 28 Nov 1852 in Effingham, Illinois, USA. She was born in 1828 in Effingham, Illinois. She died on 26 Nov 1910 in Bates County, Missouri.

George Washington Phifer and Ellen Townsend had the following children:

27. i. CHRISTINA[17] PHIFER-EWING was born in 1853 in Effingham, Effingham, Illinois, USA. She died in 1928. She married HENRY HARVEY EWING. He was born on 31 Mar 1848 in Wood, Virginia. He died on 10 Mar 1942 in Deer Creek, Bates, Missouri, USA.

ii. WILLIAM A. OR URIAH PHIFER was born in 1858. He died in 1945.

iii. FLORA E. PHIFER-STUBBLEFIELD was born in 1861. She died in 1943 in Bates County, Missouri.

iv. HANNAH PHIFER was born in 1863. She died in 1888 in Bates County, Missouri.

v. FANNY PHIFER was born in 1864.

vi. LEWIS PHIFER was born in 1865. He died in 1865.

Generation 16 (cont.)

vii. MARY ANGELINE PHIFER-HOYT was born in 1868. She died in 1949 in Bates County, Missouri.

viii. GEORGE W. PHIFER JR. was born in 1870. He died in 1965.

ix. LAURA LILLIAN PHIFER-EWING was born in 1872 in Bates County, Missouri. She died in 1966 in California.

Generation 17

27. **CHRISTINA**[17] **PHIFER-EWING** (George Washington[16] Phifer, Susan[15] Lindsey-Phifer, William S.[14] Lindsey, James[13] Lindsay, William Alexander Malcolm[12] Lindsay, Alexander III[11] Lindsay, Alexander II[10] Lindsay, Alexander[9] Lindsay, James[8] Lindsay, Patrick[7] Lindsay, John[6] Lindsay, Walter Thomas[5] Lindsay, David[4] Lindsay, Walter[3] Lindsay, David[2] Lindsay, David[1] Lindsay) was born in 1853 in Effingham, Effingham, Illinois, USA. She died in 1928. She married **HENRY HARVEY EWING**. He was born on 31 Mar 1848 in Wood, Virginia. He died on 10 Mar 1942 in Deer Creek, Bates, Missouri, USA.

Henry Harvey Ewing and Christina Phifer-Ewing had the following children:

28. i. LAURA ELLA[18] EWING was born on 14 Sep 1877 in Effingham, Effingham, Illinois, USA. She died on 29 Aug

Generation 17 (cont.)

1953 in Butler, Bates County, Missouri. She married (1) LEWIS ALVIN DURBIN on 11 Dec 1898 in Effingham, Effingham, Illinois, USA. He was born in 1877 in Effingham, Effingham, Illinois, USA. He died on 18 May 1938 in Adrian, Bates County, Missouri. She married an unknown spouse on 11 Dec 1898 in Altamont, Illinois.

ii. LILIAN FLORENCE EWING was born on 24 Dec 1882 in Moccasin, Effingham. She died in 1965 in Bates County, Missouri.

iii. MARY VIVIAN EWING was born on 26 Feb 1889 in Effingham, Illinois. She died in 1980 in California.

Generation 18

28. **LAURA ELLA**[18] **EWING** (Christina[17] Phifer-Ewing, George Washington[16] Phifer, Susan[15] Lindsey-Phifer, William S.[14] Lindsey, James[13] Lindsay, William Alexander Malcolm[12] Lindsay, Alexander III[11] Lindsay, Alexander II[10] Lindsay, Alexander[9] Lindsay, James[8] Lindsay, Patrick[7] Lindsay, John[6] Lindsay, Walter Thomas[5] Lindsay, David[4] Lindsay, Walter[3] Lindsay, David[2] Lindsay, David[1] Lindsay) was born on 14 Sep 1877 in Effingham, Effingham, Illinois, USA. She died on 29 Aug 1953 in Butler, Bates County, Missouri. She married (1) **LEWIS**

Generation 18 (cont.)

ALVIN DURBIN on 11 Dec 1898 in Effingham, Effingham, Illinois, USA. He was born in 1877 in Effingham, Effingham, Illinois, USA. He died on 18 May 1938 in Adrian, Bates County, Missouri. She married an unknown spouse on 11 Dec 1898 in Altamont, Illinois.

Laura Ella Ewing had the following child:

29. i. NELLIE[19] BARKLEY was born on 06 Aug 1900 in Cass County, Archie, Missouri. She died on 27 Oct 1948 in Shawnee, Bates County, Missouri.

Lewis Alvin Durbin and Laura Ella Ewing had the following children:

i. LESLIE ALVIN[19] DURBIN was born on 11 Oct 1908 in Bates County, Missouri. He died on 27 Sep 1952 in Adrian, Bates County, Missouri.

ii. JESSE WILLIAM DURBIN was born in 1911 in Bates County, Missouri.

iii. UFA HENRY DURBIN.

Generation 19

29. **NELLIE[19] BARKLEY** (Laura Ella[18] Ewing, Christina[17] Phifer-Ewing, George Washington[16] Phifer, Susan[15] Lindsey-Phifer, William S.[14] Lindsey, James[13] Lindsay, William Alexander Malcolm[12] Lindsay, Alexander III[11] Lindsay, Alexander II[10] Lindsay, Alexander[9] Lindsay,

Generation 19 (cont.)

James[8] Lindsay, Patrick[7] Lindsay, John[6] Lindsay, Walter Thomas[5] Lindsay, David[4] Lindsay, Walter[3] Lindsay, David[2] Lindsay, David[1] Lindsay) was born on 06 Aug 1900 in Cass County, Archie, Missouri. She died on 27 Oct 1948 in Shawnee, Bates County, Missouri.

Nellie Barkley had the following children:

i. MARVIN DARRELL DURBIN was born in 1924 in Bates County, Missouri. He died in 1992 in Seattle, Washinton.

ii. JACK CALVIN DURBIN was born on 23 Sep 1925 in Bates County, Missouri. He died in 2012 in Wichita, Sedgwick, Kansas, USA.

iii. LEONARD LEROY DURBIN was born on 20 Aug 1927 in Archie, Cass, Missouri. He died in 1995 in Butler, Bates County, Missouri.

iv. BETTY JEWELL DURBIN was born on 02 Feb 1931 in Shawnee, Bates County, Missouri. She married WINFRED LEE CARSON SR..

v. DORIS MAY DURBIN was born on 11 Aug 1932 in Adrian, Missouri (Shawnee Twp, Bates County, Missouri). She died in Manvel, Brazoria, Texas (Ashes scattered, Happy, Texas). She married Ovid

Generation 19 (cont.)

Maurice Wooley, son of Ovid Garlington Wooley and Mildred Maurine Walker, on 17 Feb 1952 in Wichita, Sedgwick, Kansas, USA (At home of brother Jack & Maedean.). He was born on 03 Jul 1933 in Happy, Texas. He died on 05 Nov 2004 in Caynon, Happy, Texas.

Notes for Doris May Durbin: Cremated, ashes scattered on old home place, Happy, Texas.

vi. PEGGY JOYCE DURBIN was born on 02 Jul 1936 in Shawnee, Bates County, Missouri. She married IRVIN LEE BEERY.

vii. CAROL JEAN DURBIN was born on 01 Jul 1940 in Shawnee, Bates County, Missouri. She married Arthur Bidner on 03 Mar 1962 in Kansas City, Missouri. He was born on 17 Feb 1932 in Brooklyn, New York.

Index of Individuals

Index of Individuals

Index of Individuals

Heritage Books by the author:

Badens in America

Barber/Barbour Genealogy: Samuel Barber, The Immigrant 1655–1704

Barber/Barbour Genealogy: Thomas Barber, The Immigrant 1614–1662

The Brice Family Who Settled in Fairfield County, South Carolina, about 1785 and Related Families

Descendants of Thomas Mattingly: Born 1623, Omny, Sussex, England. Death 24 July 1664, Newton, Charles, Maryland

Durbin and Logsdon Genealogy with Related Families, 1626–1991

The Durbin and Logsdon Genealogy with Related Families, 1626–1991, Volume 2

Durbin and Logsdon Genealogy with Related Families, 1626–1994

Durbin and Logsdon Genealogy with Related Families, 1626–1998

Durbin DNA: Connections for Betty Jewell Durbin Carson, Parents through 5th Grandparents

Durbin-Logsdon Genealogy and Related Families from Maryland to Kentucky, Volumes 1–2

CD: The Durbin and Logsdon Genealogy with Related Families, 1626–2000, 3rd Revised Edition

From D'Aubigny of Normandy, France to Robert Durbin of England and Thomas Christoper Durbin of Baltimore, Maryland

History of the Barclay/Barkley Clan

History of Curtis Land, 1635–1683; with Excerpt on Francis Land

Jean (John) Gaston of France

John Thomas Carson (1520–1570) Down County, Northern Ireland

Lindsay/Lindsey Royalty Connections from Charlemagne to Kings of Scotland

MacKenzie Clan of the Ancient Celtic MacAlpine Line of Scottish Kings from the Original Anglo-Saxon Kings of England, 1160 to 1751

Our Ewing Heritage, with Related Families, Part One and Two, Revised Edition
Betty Jewell Durbin Carson and Doris M. Durbin Wooley

CD: Our Ewing Heritage, with Related Families, Revised Edition
Betty Jewell Durbin Carson and Doris M. Durbin Wooley

Patterson Family History

www.ingramcontent.com/pod-product-compliance
Lightning Source LLC
LaVergne TN
LVHW020632100826
845148LV00012B/2145